Curriculum
and Assessment Guides
for Infant and Child Care

Curriculum and Assessment Guides for Infant and Child Care

WILLIAM FOWLER

The Ontario Institute for Studies in Education

Allyn and Bacon, Inc.

BOSTON   LONDON   SYDNEY   TORONTO

Portions of this book first appeared in *Infant and Child Care: A Guide to Education in Group Settings* by William Fowler. Copyright © 1980 by Allyn and Bacon, Inc.

Library of Congress Cataloguing in Publication Data

Fowler, William,
    Curriculum and assessment guides for infant and child care.

    Includes index.
    1. Child development—Study and teaching.
2. Education, Preschool—Curricula.   3. Day Care centers.   I. Title.
HQ755.7.F67   372.21   79–15435
ISBN 0-205-06537-6

Printed in the Unites States of America.

Contents

Preface

Detailed curriculum guides and assessment devices are relatively recent tools in infant and preschool education, principally because caring for young children in groups is in itself comparatively new. Nursery schools have been around since the turn of the century, but have generally excluded infants and been limited in numbers, serving mainly university middle-class communities or the welfare clients of social agencies. Group day care got its start with the sudden inclusion of significant numbers of women in the work force during World War II, again enrolling mainly children over two. Day care centers declined in number in the early postwar era when the social ideology of the period drew women back into the home.

Both nursery school practice and the early forms of group day care, which initially attempted to pattern itself after the nursery school model, were concerned more with the health and development of the whole child in informal play programs than with detailed learning sequences and program-related assessments. This orientation was in keeping with the conceptions and goals of nursery schools (as the name implies) as either part-time play environments for children of the affluent or part- or full-time play environments for children from broken homes or similar circumstances—children who needed special supplementary care and opportunities to play. While there were exceptions, and university-sponsored or related institutions often conducted extensive research on young children, much of it was devoted to charting profiles of adjustment and development in terms of norms.

It has only been with the advent of group day care on a large scale, its extension to infancy, the focus on all-day care for working mothers, and, above all, the growth of awareness of the significant role that early cognitive experience serves in development that serious attention to educational program development and assessment has appeared. The present set of curriculum and evaluation materials are an outgrowth of these developments and outlook.

The curriculum guides present a comprehensive series of concept learning sequences, while the assessment guides provide multiple scales for evaluating the child, the teacher/caregiver, and the program characteristics on both cognitive and socioemotional processes. Systematic attention to cognitive learning in the early years is as vital for healthy development as are general care and play. If little children are to be widely cared for for long hours every day in groups and not merely for a few hours in play groups, we cannot leave to chance the foundation of their intellectual skills and interests, any more than we can their socioemotional life. It is important to note that structuring curriculum sequences systematically is not to be confused with methods of teaching. The former takes account of the fact that concepts are inherently different in complexity. Organizing them in steps along a sequence of difficulty, therefore, makes it easier for the child to learn, a step at a time. Teaching methods, on the other hand, need to be informal and fluid, fostering initiative and spontaneity in interacting with the material and the teacher.

The guides were developed over the course of longitudinal research projects in nursery school and group day care settings, chief of which was a three-year study in a private agency[1] and a five-year study in a municipal center of Metro Toronto.[2] The guides have been employed in various ways in the different programs and settings as described in the instructions accompanying each guide. Each of the guides has thus progressed through a series of steps in its development, undergoing modifications as experience indicated, culminating with the present completed versions.

Both the curriculum guides—knowledge, problem solving, language, or toy—and the assessment techniques can be employed singly in almost any program and setting of group care and education. Similarly, each of the assessment techniques measures different functions of children and program, which while certainly interrelated, provide independent information and insights useful for modifying different aspects of the methods and conditions of care. The first of the two evaluation instruments focuses on the individual child, how she/he is progressing in (or a given caregiver/teacher is fostering) development (Diagnostic-Developmental Monitoring System) on a variety of cognitive, motivational and socioemotional processes. The second is a comprehensive series of scales for evaluating all aspects of a school or care environment and program (Environmental Profile).

Selected learning sequences or scales and clusters or subsets of the various sequences and scales can, moreover, be used singly or in combination, according to need or preference, even though reliability values reported apply to the total instrument in each case, except where indicated.

Many people have influenced or aided me in the development of these guides in various ways—theorists, fellow researchers and teachers, students, caregivers, parents, and children. I would like especially to thank researchers and students who made particular contributions to the assessment guides: Nasim Khan for his extensive collaboration in revising and testing the Diagnostic-Developmental Monitoring System, and Karen Ogston for collaborating in revising and testing the Environmental Profile.

[1] Fowler, W. "A Developmental Learning Approach to Infant Care in a Group Setting," *Merrill-Palmer Quarterly,* 1972, *18,* 145–175.

[2] Fowler, W. "Day Care and Its Effects on Early Development: A Study of Group and Home Care in Multi-Ethnic, Working Class Families," Toronto: Ontario Institute for Studies in Education, 1978.

Introduction to Project Curriculum Guides: Knowledge Curriculum, Problem Solving Curriculum, and Language Curriculum

HOW THE GUIDES ARE ORGANIZED AND USED

The curriculum guides that follow provide outlines of cognitive learning activities and teaching techniques for each of three primary concept areas: knowledge, problem solving, and language. While each of the guides follows a slightly different form, each is organized in terms of major concepts and rules that are useful and in some ways essential for children to learn during early development. Thus in knowledge concepts, the list embraces basic concepts about the material world and how it works; in problem solving, concept strategies of how to solve and carry out tasks; and in language, the complex rules by which ideas are coded and manipulated in abstract forms. Similarly, each of the curricula contains a description of appropriate materials, techniques, and activities for learning the concepts.

Each of the curricula is also organized according to different concept areas and sequenced according to levels of difficulty. The difficulty levels are determined by the number of elements and the complexity of relations involved in the concept. For example, in knowledge concepts, comparisons of two sizes are easier than comparisons of three or more in a series; in problem solving, tools with a single part are easier to master than those with several interacting parts; and in language, of course, words that stand for things (nouns) are easier to learn than words describing things (adjectives). The concept area divisions are partly a matter of convenience, for example, barrier problems versus tool-using in problem solving, and partly a question of differences in level, as in learning about objects versus learning about groups (sets or classes) of things in knowledge concepts.

For each level in a series there is a *suggested age range* for teaching the concepts. Note, however, that the range covers the period for *starting* to teach at the level concerned. The ranges indicated are necessarily broad, since much depends on how much the infant or child already knows. The abilities of children vary enormously at each age, but more important is the fact that children of the same age have been stimulated to different degrees and in different concepts. Thus, estimates need to be made of the child's level of attainment in each concept area before the guides can be applied effectively. The child's skills, or lack of skills in related areas, may not be immediately evident in trying out his/her competence in specific concepts, and later may require adjustment up or down in level.

The age ranges indicated embrace a wide range of extremes of ability— from the advanced infant, who would begin close to the earliest age indicated for the level, to children from unstimulating backgrounds, who would begin at the oldest age indicated for the level. It is possible, in fact likely, that some children could not begin a level until past the upper age limit indicated; others might start earlier with some simple form of the concepts for the level (though the lower limits are already quite advanced). There is no substitute for flexibility. In the final analysis these curriculum sequences, and especially the age ranges, are *guidelines* that need to be adapted and individualized for each child according to his/her level, style, and rate of—and of course interest in—learning.

Note that the three curriculum guides are intended to provide a comprehensive outline of a major body of concepts useful for children to learn during early development. Because the variety of such concepts is extensive and complex, the list of concepts is lengthy and the techniques are presented in considerable detail. But as every teacher and caregiver knows, lengthy written guides can be unwieldy to employ in everyday teaching with young children. How then can they be used?

There are few problems when employed to teach principles of child care and learning in teacher-caregiver educational settings. The guides are particularly fashioned to be used for discussions on guiding children's learning. Whether in educational settings for day care teachers or through inservice training activities in laboratory type day care and nursery school settings, the time available and the interest in quality and experimentation makes comprehensive guides ideal.

But these guides also lend themselves to everyday use in ordinary child care and school settings, in fact, because of the detail of concept sequences and techniques provided. They are convenient planning aids for preparing actual learning activities. They can be used more or less as is, to work on various concepts with children according to their readiness levels for the different concepts. Usually an overall plan for the center will be needed in which different aspects of each of the three concept areas are presented each week to all children on some alternating basis. Group planning and coordination with the aid of the supervisor and leadership staff (in larger centers) are obviously helpful. While overplanning and scheduling can result in losing sight of children's needs and a general stifling of spontaneity for children and staff alike, lack of attention to curriculum planning and coordination produces disorganization, unevenness, and usually boring programs for children. The best quality child care strikes a balance between informality and planning of the care and learning activities. Such balance is usually developed best through daily use of the guides.

The quickest and most valuable method to employ guides is by combining them (in brief form as concept learning goals) in a chart for recording children's progress. This way brings the teaching process down to earth, putting it in a form that individualizes a plan and focuses the guide on the actual teaching and learning process in a single record system. Single-page concept guides, perhaps organized in a series in looseleaf notebooks, with sections for each child, constitute a flexible, ready reference system that can be kept at hand to be used with the learning materials in a guided learning area. Further details on using the curriculum are presented with each guide.

1

Knowledge Curriculum

GENERAL CHARACTERISTICS

Everything we do rests on knowledge. We cannot carry out any task or even move from one place to another without some knowledge about the nature of things, the variety and types of objects, and how things relate to one another and move and change in space and time. Knowledge is one of the three basic categories of concepts that enables us to function in everyday life.

The knowledge curriculum is aimed at furthering the development of young children's basic repertoire of these concepts of the nature of things. The emphasis is on the general form of things and processes rather than on particular information content such as types of animals, buildings or trees. Thus the focus is that any objects can be classified into types, rather than the groupings of, for instance, dishes or stamps themselves.

Developing the child's fund of general information is of course just as important as developing his/her understanding of basic rules of how things work. The sheltered residential life of the suburbs is as vulnerable to dwarfing the child's range of information in one way as life in poverty in the inner city is in another. Day care itself and schools can be colored with a sameness and ritual of experience that narrows the child's awareness of the wider community. Thus knowledge about the content of the world, both of the everyday social environment and of things uncommon to the child's experience, needs supplementary direct experience in different community settings, along with a generous amount of picture story activity. The strategy recommended here for ensuring that children in schools and day care encounter a rich variety of content experiences is the organization of sectors of care and educational activities into common theme projects. General information is nicely imparted through a little extra planning and coordinating of trips and stories with sociodramatic and creative play.

Basic cognitive concepts are achieved more easily, on the other hand, through a different kind of planning and setting. It is of course true that considerable basic knowledge about dimensions and other concepts, such as the features and functions of furniture, clothes, and people, is acquired through everyday experience and trips, stories, and theme programs. But unlike the content of, for example, the movement of an eggbeater or the filtering of a sieve, the idea that *both* eggbeaters *and* sieves do special things (perform specific functions) is more general and abstract. Children often acquire such knowledge more easily and with greater clarity and organization in relatively quiet and isolated settings, where material can be presented more selectively and systematically. Their attention needs to be concentrated on the particular features of selected tools or other objects in order to compare their characteristics and see how those objects function in the specialized ways that they are designed to work. Clutter, distraction, and the presence of objects whose size or position of the features makes the point less obvious need to be avoided. Moreover, such abstract concepts are linked together in complex structures that require simplification and sorting out in abstract manipulations before the little child can make substantial headway.

Actually, progress in complex understanding of knowledge in any information area is dependent on a knowledge of these formal rules about the nature of things. For example, knowledge of the nature of ships and boats and how they are classified involves such basic concepts as counting and measurement (linear, area, and volume), dimensional concepts of size (magnitude); multiple hierarchical classification (ships are grouped in many types, such as sailing and mechanical power, and levels, such as mechanical powered vessels may include diesel, steam turbine, or gasoline, and gasoline engines may be inboard or outboard), and many others. Basic knowledge concepts *are* complex, but the young child can grasp many of the rules about them if they are simplified and presented a step or two at a time in some logical order of difficulty and if he/she is shown and has plenty of opportunity to experiment with a wide variety of examples. How well the child learns these concepts and how many of them he/she learns depends on the amount of time and care furnished in a sequenced program of this type.

The outline of knowledge concepts that follows is organized along these lines. There are four basic levels of complexity, each of which is composed of a number of component levels and types of concepts. These levels are a matter of convenience as well as difficulty. In other words, as the suggested age ranges marked in the right hand column indicate, many of the levels overlap and may be taught concurrently. In fact, many of the difficulties of teaching and learning arise from the fact that concepts are usually closely interrelated in different ways at various levels. Even the general order of the four levels is not rigidly fixed. Concepts about processes and change at Level IV for example, are logically introduced beginning early in infancy in the form of attention to simple movements, and the means and ends of doing things with the hands, right along with learning about the permanence of objects and object characteristics at Level I. Levels and types are thus greatly intertwined, and selected sections of the guide can readily be varied in many ways according to each child's needs and to some extent according to teacher preference.

There is nevertheless a logic to the order, which is found as much or more in the sequences of difficulty specified for the various types of concepts within the levels (e.g., object permanence or material characteristics at Level I, Object Structures) as in the sequences between the major levels. It is wise, therefore, to form some plan for sampling all areas of the curriculum over a period of time and at the same time work with the child along the sequence of difficulty for each area and type indicated by the order and age ranges.

For each level and type, four kinds of information are presented, outlined in column form. The major concept categories, such as object structures, and the main subcategories, such as object recognition and spatial construction of objects, are presented across the top of the page in major headings and subheadings. Under each heading, the various types of concepts within each category are then listed in the column at the left. Each concept listed on the left is accompanied by brief statements of the *rules* that define the concept in general terms and under various specific conditions. The aim of the program is to guide teachers in techniques that will help the child understand these rules. Concepts become part of a child only when she/he understands their general meaning through action. The child must know how concepts work in terms of specific action rules. Otherwise concepts become empty labels that the child cannot apply from one situation to the next. Concepts are abstractions about regularities that are found only by applying rules to handle things selectively. Identifying the color red, for example, or brightness involves picking objects according to the single quality of redness or the intensity of light; in each case the rule states (or implies) that other characteristics, such as size or weight, should be ignored. Thus, the child comes to understand these abstract concept regularities by playing with patterns of objects according to such rules.

The remaining three columns contain, in order from left to right, suggestions for materials that are convenient for teaching each concept, lists of teaching techniques, and in the last column on the right, the suggested ages to begin a given concept. Many different materials may of course be used to teach the same concept, and the same set of materials will work for many different concepts. Things that vary in size, for instance, often vary in color, shape, and weight. They only have to be manipulated in different ways to illustrate the different rules. In order to teach concepts broadly and abstractly it is important that enough different materials are available to show how the rules for each concept can be applied to a broad range of particular materials. In order to minimize preparation time each day and to make the teaching and learning situation smooth and enjoyable for both caregiver and child, it is advisable to prepare several kits of materials, placing them on shelves for ready use.

The *techniques* on how to teach each concept in column three are composed of both general guidelines for an area or type of concept and specific points for demonstrating the rules under various conditions. Again the aim is for the child to manipulate materials in particular ways that point up the rules and to see many different examples with the same rules to help her/him generalize.*

These general principles and methods are incorporated in various ways,

* Detailed discussion of the general principles and methods for guiding concept learning have been developed in William Fowler, *Infant and Child Care* (Boston: Allyn and Bacon, 1980), Chs. 10–14, Appendix A.

as appropriate, into the specific instructions on technique. (A comparatively comprehensive, brief outline of methods is contained in the list of methods for teaching object recognition, presented near the beginning of the curriculum in Section IB, page 11).

As noted above, *suggested ages* at which a broad range of children are likely to be ready to begin to learn the respective concepts are presented in the right-hand column of the guide. But once again, devote a few trials to diagnosing each child's competencies accurately and be flexible in shifting among the concepts and levels as needed.

I. OBJECT STRUCTURES

> **Identity and characteristics of objects.**

A. PERMANENCE OF OBJECTS (IDENTITY)

> *Objects have a separate and relatively permanent existence independent of our senses.*

Concepts and Rules	Materials	How to Teach	Age to Begin (Mos.)
General			
Objects continue to exist under all kinds of conditions	A variety of small, appealing objects—from simple shapes of one color (e.g., red ball or block) to things with many colors, sounds, and other features (e.g., dolls, blocks, clocks).	Attract and maintain the infant's attention to many different objects through presenting things in various interesting actions related to his/her sight, sound, and touch; name the objects and actions frequently, timing your language to fit your movements.	0–3
Such *Specific Conditions* as:	Same	Show infant moving objects and move objects across infant's view:	0–3
1. When they move around in local space, i.e., close at hand (proximal space)		a. at different speeds (always start slowly). b. in different directions (change from horizontal to vertical, to angular, to circular movements). c. at different distances (about 6 to 40 inches, 15 to 100 centimeters) toward and away from infant.	
2. When perceived through different senses, separately and together (multiple sensory motor development and integration)	Same	Shift objects around to involve the different senses (mainly sight, touch, and hearing) and in shifting order and combinations (e.g., place in his hand the objects moved before his eye, and vice versa; make noise with moving objects, etc.).	0–4

I. OBJECT STRUCTURES (cont.)

Concepts and Rules	Materials	How to Teach	Age to Begin (Mos.)
3. When they disappear *Negation and nothing*: the disappearance of objects begins the idea of negating something and no object (nothing) left.	Same *Plus*: A variety of screens and barriers (e.g., boxes, cloth, shelves, cardboard, blocks, pillows, toys, furniture, the child, teacher, etc.); any convenient object, movable or immovable which is large enough to screen hidden objects.	Hide a variety of objects behind different screens at varied angles from child and in immediate view of child, progressing through a series of steps: 1. Partial to total hiding. 2. Total hiding. 3. Hiding behind the last of two to four screens in a series, visibly so child can see both object and hand movements. 4. Moving objects in a path that goes behind a screen to emerge at the other side, varying speed and angle of pathway. 5. Similar to No. 3, but with object hidden in hand.	2–4
4. When they move away, around, or disappear at a distance (distal space)	Same	Move objects away from, toward, and around infant, and hide objects at gradually increasing distances (3 to 10+ feet, 1 to 3+ meters) in the same manner as was done with the infant close at hand.	4–6

B. RECOGNITION OF OBJECTS

> *Recognizing objects by their features and material characteristics.*

Concepts and Rules	Materials	How to Teach	Age to Begin (Mos.)
General Objects can be distinguished from one another in a number of ways:	A wide variety of objects and pictures, varying in both categories of information (e.g., people, animals,	Present objects to be learned as an inquiry and search game of *analyzing* and *relating* (synthesizing) characteristics by teacher and child, separately and jointly: 1. Objects which are contrasted on selected features and characteristics.	0–36

continued

I. OBJECT STRUCTURES (cont.)

Concepts and Rules	Materials	How to Teach	Age to Begin (Mos.)

	plants, vehicles, dishes, etc.) and types of material characteristics (e.g., color, shape, etc.). Use many miniature replicas but also small and large real objects.
	
	Special miniature toys (dolls, people, animals, furniture, tools, vehicles) for sociodramatic play.
		2. Comparing objects (mainly) in pairs on relevant features and characteristics:
		
		  a. Discriminated for differences.
		  b. Matched for similarities.
		
		3. In a wide variety of situations.
		4. With different examples of the same types of objects, features, and characteristics.
		5. Using well-defined, aesthetically pleasing examples.
		6. Generally, against a flat, unpatterned background of uniform, contrasting color.
		7. In a variety of teacher-infant interactive sensory motor, sociodramatic play, and problem-solving activities.
		8. Using language freely, but simply and expressively, to describe objects and activities, timing use of labels to your movements and the infant's attention. Expect the child to discriminate (point to) and identify (name) requested items only gradually as understanding and language develop.
		9. Interesting the infant by showing pleasure in his efforts and the activities (avoid criticism).
		10. Sequencing the order of difficulty as follows, pacing according to infant's progress:
		
		  a. Simple to complex objects (increasing number and intricacy of features).
		  b. Teach recognition of one or two objects (feature or characteristic) at a time, adding new ones only as the preceding item is well learned.
		  c. Single to multiple object/feature-characteristic recognition (in a session).
			0–36

I. OBJECT STRUCTURES (cont.)

Concepts and Rules	Materials	How to Teach	Age to Begin (Mos.)
		d. Objects then pictures, frequently relating pictures to similar objects. e. Demonstrating and labeling—discriminating (asking child to point to one of two different objects/features-characteristics)—identifying (asking child to name)—matching (similar objects). f. Common (familiar) to less common (unfamiliar) objects.	0–36
In Such Specific Ways as: 1. *Globally* (whole object recognition)	A limited number of relatively simple objects (as above).	Essentially the same as general model, but stick to a few simple objects until the child begins to grasp named objects on request.	0–6
By their 2. (a) *Specific Features* (designed characteristics)	Like general model: numerous examples of functional objects (objects that have a purpose) either natural (e.g., animals and plants) or human made (e.g., tools and household objects).	Essentially the same. Begin indicating and naming object features as soon as the infant begins to recognize a few objects. Start with prominent features of simple, familiar objects and limit focus to two or three new features in a several-minute teaching session.	2–8
(b) and *Functions* (structural-functional relations: what the objects and features do).	Same as for features, but use only features whose actions are fairly visible.	Essentially the same. The *functions* of many features can be taught about as early as the features themselves. The functions of objects and of their features need to be clearly (and often repeatedly) demonstrated, however, by simple actions. Actions are essentially processes (see later section, Level IV, on Processes), more abstract because they are visible only in passing while they occur. *Structural-functional relations*: It is important to pick objects and features with	4–8

continued

I. OBJECT STRUCTURES (cont.)

Concepts and Rules	Materials	How to Teach	Age to Begin (Mos.)
		functions that are comparatively obvious and direct (e.g., the functions of the wheels and seats of a car would be easier to illustrate than those of the engine). Pick features that have shapes or other characteristics that bear a clear relation to the functions they are designed to perform (e.g., the carrying section of a truck, bulb from a lamp, point of a crayon). Draw the infant's attention to these characteristics and comment on them *briefly* to show relations between structural characteristics and functions.	4–8
		Object features and functions are taught throughout development. Once the basic concepts of feature and function are assimilated in infancy, learning should extend across a broad range of new areas at increasingly complex levels.	
By their 3. *Material Characteristics* (intrinsic properties) such as:		Follows basic model. Except for shape, material characteristics are initially taught by using pairs of objects contrasting sharply on the relevant characteristic (e.g., red versus blue or rough versus smooth). Defer teaching characteristics in terms of degrees of difference in a scaled sequence until later in development (see Section III.A: Seriation).	8–24
a. *Shape*	Like general model: numerous examples of objects convenient to illustrate variations in shape and contour.		
		Essentially the same. Prominent aspects of shape (e.g., roundness of balls and wheels, squareness of boxes, sharp angles) can be taught along with specific features. Begin with clear examples of circles (e.g., geometric shapes, toys, wheels, balls) and squares (e.g., geometric shapes, toys, and boxes), gradually introducing less clear examples and more complex shapes (e.g.,	8–18

I. OBJECT STRUCTURES (cont.)

Concepts and Rules	Materials	How to Teach	Age to Begin (Mos.)
		triangles, diamonds, other polygons, ovals, curves, flat, angles—right and acute, etc.)	8–18
		Draw attention to characteristic features of shapes (e.g., continuous roundness of circles, sharp angles of triangles).	
b. *Color* Type	Like general model: all kinds of objects representing the spectrum of basic colors and intermediate hues and shades.	Essentially the same. First teach major colors (red, yellow, blue, green, orange, purple) in clear, bright examples. Then teach brown, black, white, gray and gradually variations in brightness and saturation for all colors (e.g., pink, lavender, light blue).	12–18
c. *Light* Volume (intensity) (bright-dim; light-dark).	A variety of objects that give light (flashlights, lamps, candles, etc.).	Essentially the same. Use similar and different sources of light in pairs at different levels of brightness and degrees of difference. Care must be exercised not to shine bright lights directly at the child, nor to frighten the child when contrasts between dark and light are presented.	12–18
d. *Sound* (1) Type (2) Volume (loud and soft) (3) Pitch (high-low) (4) Duration (short-long)	A variety of noise-making objects and musical instruments, including bottles, metal pipes, bamboo sticks, etc., making different tones.	Essentially the same, but pairs of sounds and tones are usually presented in succession over time, introducing the problem of memory and greater abstractness. Sounds are thus processes (see Section IV) but are included here (and later under seriation, Section IIIA) because they appear as characteristics of objects). Teach a variety of types of sounds and tones with different objects, using appropriate labels, like bang (block), ring (bell), buzz (buzzer), blowing sounds (air, wind), hum, talk, song (voice), music (instruments), roar (animals, engines), bark (dog), etc.; use many sounds of musical instruments and singing as examples, naming the instruments.	12–18

continued

I. OBJECT STRUCTURES (cont.)

Concepts and Rules	Materials	How to Teach	Age to Begin (Mos.)
		Present pairs of sounds that vary alternately in volume, pitch, duration, etc. to different degrees.	12–18
		Vary distance and direction in many ways.	
		Avoid sudden noises that startle, intensely irritating sounds (e.g., intense grinding or high-pitched screeching sounds), or too loud sounds that may frighten.	
e. *Textures* (surface characteristics)	Like general model: numerous examples of objects convenient to illustrate variations in texture.	Essentially the same. Teach obvious contrasts of texture (e.g., rough-smooth, hard-soft, wet-dry, even-uneven, sticky-dry), gradually introducing less obvious qualities (e.g., spongy, rubbery, soapy, greasy, webbed).	12–18
		The child needs to touch and feel materials extensively.	
f. *Temperature*	Use only a few examples showing obvious variations in temperature (e.g., ice, cold water, juice, metal, air; **hot** water, milk, food, air, metal, sand).	Essentially the same, but introduce only a few contrasting pairs of *moderately* hot and cold objects to explore at this stage.	12–18
		Be careful to avoid touching hot objects. Use the teaching situation as a means of beginning to develop *rational* respect for extremes of heat (including fire) and cold. Teach extremes by getting near enough (not too close) to feel the radiation, by showing how things burn (e.g., paper, wood) or boil and freeze (e.g., water, juice) and by drawing attention to (and commenting on) extremes of weather—and how we protect ourselves (e.g., clothes changes, heat and cool houses).	
		Avoid fearful or anxious attitudes in talking about dangers. Avoid temperatures extreme enough to induce pain or frighten the infant. Hot objects he/she touches should really be only quite warm and the cold, quite cool—except for ice, which should *not* be placed in the mouth, for fear of swallowing.	

I. OBJECT STRUCTURES (cont.)

Concepts and Rules	*Materials*	*How to Teach*	*Age to Begin (Mos.)*
g. *Taste and Smell* (1) Type (2) Intensity (strong-weak flavor or smell)	All sorts of age-appropriate foods that vary in taste and foods and other natural and artificial substances (e.g., flowers, perfume, cleaning agents, etc.).	Essentially the same.	8–14

Taste and smell are often conveniently taught in the same context because much of taste experience is contributed by odors, although there are differences.

Meal and snack times are ideal occasions to teach about taste/smell experiences, using the ordinary foods of his/her diet. When extended to play learning experiences in tasting adult foods on special occasions, these experiences are likely to develop a broader, more adaptive style in the enjoyment of food.

The following are major types of taste labels, most of which are also associated with characteristic smells; they vary in intensity, but are taught most easily first in terms of presence or absence, i.e., "Is it _____ ?"

sweet	salty
sour (acid)	spicy (e.g., pepper)
bitter	fruity
meaty	chocolate
burned	perfume
greasy (oily)	nutty

Certain types can be compared in terms of contrasting opposites, i.e., sweet versus sour, sweet versus bitter; but nearly all can be compared (contrasted or matched) in many different pair combinations. Because the list of substances with distinct odors and foods and food dishes with distinct flavors and fragrances is virtually endless among many cultures, refinement of taste/smell concepts can continue over many years.

Have the infant taste and smell alternately the same substance, where possible and *not* harmful. Later, use the experience to

continued

I. OBJECT STRUCTURES (cont.)

Concepts and Rules	Materials	How to Teach	Age to Begin (Mos.)
		mention that some things are poisonous (make him sick) or not good for him/her, but don't illustrate (except through picture stories)—and watch out for hot things (see Section I.B.f. on Temperature). Be definite but matter of fact, not alarmist or anxious.	8–14
h. *Substances* (composition of materials)	Like general model: numerous examples of objects that clearly illustrate types of material substances.	Essentially the same. Teach no more than a few basic substances in the early stages (e.g., metal, wood, glass, plastic, cotton), using examples that contrast well with one another.	18–24
		Avoid concern for scientific accuracy and hierarchical classification (see Section III.B): thus the child may accept two labels for one substance: metal and iron. Merely develop awareness of composition and a few common labels; because substances tend to get confused with object names, they are sometimes difficult to learn.	

C. THE CONSTRUCTION OF OBJECTS IN SPACE

> *Organization and relations.*

Concepts and Rules	Materials	How to Teach	Age to Begin (Mos.)
Objects are organized and interrelated in space.	A variety of common, movable objects of different sizes, shapes and color as in I.B.; use pictures in which spatial relations are clearly drawn.	Point to, name, and ask about simple spatial aspects *of* and *between* objects in the course of planned, casual, and physical caregiving activities, using the same play-oriented sensory motor discrimination and sequencing approaches defined in Section I.B.	10–18
		Use pictures to teach spatial relations, mainly: (1) when infant can readily recognize objects and features in pictures,	

I. OBJECT STRUCTURES (cont.)

Concepts and Rules	Materials	How to Teach	Age to Begin (Mos.)
		and (2) when spatial relations are clearly drawn.	10–18
		Teach concepts, mainly in polar contrast pairs. Defer teaching concepts of degree and seriation until teaching dimensions (Section III.A.).	
Specific Rules 1. *The Spatial Structure of Objects* can be defined in terms of several dimensions (coordinates)	Use mainly objects with a clear differentiation of top-bottom, sides, access to inside and sometimes under the object (e.g., a table, miniature car, or inverted box).	Use the caregiver, another child, and the infant himself/herself frequently to illustrate spatial relations to sharpen self-awareness. As in general model, teach about objects with sample contrast items of the listed dimensions in approximately the following order: a. Vertical: top-bottom; upper-lower. b. Horizontal: sides; defer left-right until other spatial concepts learned. c. Frontal: front-back; other side; face. d. Central-peripheral: center; middle; edge; corner; inner-outer (side); surface.	10–15
2. *Objects in Space*: Objects can be located in space in terms of several dimensions of structure	Same as general model, but especially small objects.	As in general model, teach external spatial relations to and between objects with sample contrast items of the listed dimensions in roughly the following order: a. Vertical: up-down; over-under; above-beneath; high-low. b. Horizontal: beside; next to; along side; defer left-right until other concepts learned. c. Frontal: before-behind; in front of-in back of. d. Position (placement): on (on top of)-off. e. Containment: in-out (inside-outside). f. Distance (proximal-distal): near-far (close to-far away). g. Direction: to (toward)-away (from). h. Intervening space: between; among. i. Barriers-detours: around; over-under; through; behind; in; on the other side.	10–15

continued

I. OBJECT STRUCTURES (cont.)

Concepts and Rules	Materials	How to Teach	Age to Begin (Mos.)
3. Part-whole Relations Objects and materials are made of parts that are related to one another and to make a whole. *Negation and Nothing* The beginning idea of negating whole sets of things and having nothing (left) begins conveniently here.	Use single objects with several parts and materials, solid and liquid, including flowing solids like sand and malleable materials like plasticene, play dough, and clay; very simple two- or three-piece puzzles and take-apart toys; food portions.	Follow general model, but emphasis is on discriminating or identifying parts (analysis) and relating them to one another and the whole object or material (integration). Guide child in taking apart and putting together plasticene, puzzles, and take-apart toys, as well as in exploring parts of toys that don't come apart. Pointing to, dividing, and talking about portions of food (e.g., desserts, vegetables, meat, milk, and juice) at meal and snack times is particularly inviting. Use such *indefinite terms* to describe part-whole relations (in both whole-object explorations and take-apart activities as:	15–18

Part

part, piece, portion, slice, section
some, any
much, little
half

Whole

all, whole
entire

Negation-nothing

none, not any
no more
nothing

More detailed and precise consideration of part-whole and quantitative relations of materials (continuous matter) and sets (discontinuous matter) will be discussed in Sections II and III.

II. GROUP STRUCTURES

> **Concrete groups and organizations: objects can be grouped and organized in local space and time.**

A. SPATIAL (PHYSICAL) GROUPS

> *Objects grouped together on the basis of physical proximity or contiguity.*

Concepts and Rules	Materials	How to Teach	Age to Begin (Mos.)
General Objects can be placed together (clustered) physically according to spatial characteristics and organization:	Building blocks of all kinds; miscellaneous collections of small to medium sized objects (2 inches to 2 feet or five to seventy centimeters on a side), covering a range of different characteristics; miniature people, vehicles, trees for sociodramatic play. Clear photographs, drawings, and diagrams of selected spatial structures.	Spatial grouping and rules of organization are best taught through *block building*, although global grouping and selected spatial concepts (e.g., linear and enclosure) can be illustrated through demonstrations and play with other materials.	10–30

The *same basic play interaction teaching methods* outlined for teaching object recognition (Section I.B.) is employed *with important variations.* That is, demonstrating, coordinated with language (i.e., naming the structure and describing its characteristics: e.g., a "line" of toys or a "bridge"—"see how one block crosses over two blocks and leaves a tunnel"); asking the child to discriminate and identify contrasting concepts (e.g., "line" versus "floor" of blocks or other toys) and to match; using different examples; showing interest, etc.

Variations: The major addition to teaching is the necessity of the child himself/herself *creating* (building) structures to represent spatial concepts. Such spatial constructions are more complicated and creative than the task of recognizing objects by features. There is a series of analyses and integrations of elements and relations between blocks that must be constructed in a certain pattern not easy to reconstruct even when a model is available to copy. *Experimentation* with

continued

II. GROUP STRUCTURES (cont.)

Concepts and Rules	Materials	How to Teach	Age to Begin (Mos.)
		the blocks in play thus contributes as much to learning spatial concepts as guidance and demonstrations by a teacher, important as the latter may be.	10–30
		Association with *sociodramatic play*. Block building lends itself strongly to social play, at least for the more advanced grouping-building concepts: use a variety of miniature figures, vehicles, etc., with which to lead and follow the child in social themes (e.g., job themes, domestic play, shopping), using the various block structures.	
		The examples and stimulation to play that other children provide, especially those slightly more skilled, is an excellent stimulus to learning.	
		Gradually introduce clear pictures and drawings of various spatial concepts for the child to discriminate and use as models, as he/she starts to master each new concept with actual objects. Diagrams and photographs can sometimes point up a relationship better than real models, once the child becomes familiar with the rules of pictorial representation.	
Specific Ways of Spatial Grouping:	Same	Same, but in a limited manner with regard to number and variety of tasks and forms of play.	
Globally (in unordered piles or clusters)		The focus is simply on the teacher and/or the infant gathering together (and describing) miscellaneous collections of objects into random clusters and piles, heaps, or mounds.	10–12
		Contrasting and matching single objects and groups are useful. Block building is too advanced for this stage.	
By Structural (Dimensional) Organization:		Essentially the same; tasks, play, and themes are still quite limited for both linear and area concepts and activities. The child's	12–30

II. GROUP STRUCTURES (cont.)

Concepts and Rules	Materials	How to Teach	Age to Begin (Mos.)
Objects can be placed together in groups in terms of three basic aspects (dimensions) that form successive levels of complexity:		interest in a play learning session is likely to focus only occasionally on the relevant concept. The child is likely to be able to discriminate (choose) between two structures (e.g., row versus floor or wall) for some time (weeks) before he can build such structures himself. Each successive dimension may require as long as several months to learn—thus do not press performance but encourage play until the three dimensional stage is attained. Block building—demonstration and play—begin here.	12–30
1. In *lines* (linear) Along a single direction (dimension): a. horizontally—rows and columns b. vertically—towers	Use objects of similar size to make the linear form clear. Towers require objects with relatively flat or matching surfaces (e.g., blocks, cups, paper, boxes) to provide vertical stability.	Essentially the same. Encourage practice with both towers and rows of blocks of different sizes and dimensions. Towers generally precede rows in development.	12–18
2. *By Area* Objects built or spread out in two directions (dimensions): a. horizontally—to cover a surface area without piling (floors). b. vertically—in the form of walls or fences.	Again use objects of similar size to point up area concepts. Walls, like towers, must also be constructed with matching surface materials (mainly blocks of all kinds).	Essentially the same. The development from making rows (and towers) to making floors or areas (and walls) comes through the child's own experimentation combined with: 1. Showing him, then asking him to show you the difference, e.g., between rows (towers) and areas (walls) of blocks placed side by side. In showing him differences, the teacher should point to and say how rows go in one direction while floors (and walls) go in two; the child, however, should be asked only to point to (not say) which is which when asked "Which is the row (or floor)?" 2. Occasionally adding a block or two at	15–24

continued

II. GROUP STRUCTURES (cont.)

Concepts and Rules	Materials	How to Teach	Age to Begin (Mos.)
		right angles to her/his row of blocks to get her/him started toward area building.	15–24
3. As *Building Structures* Constructing groups in three directions (dimensions): width, length, and height (combines floors and walls to make masses or boxlike structures).	Like towers and walls, three dimensional structures require objects with matching surfaces to make structures with vertical walls and right angles in order to construct in three dimensions.	Essentially the same, but now of course comparing the difference between rows (towers), floors (walls) and mass structures ("houses" or "buildings") in different pair combinations and adding blocks occasionally at right angles to the child's floors and walls.	18–30
And by numerous specific spatial-structural characteristics and relations.	Mainly unit and other building blocks, though other materials (especially, boxes) can be employed.	Essentially the same general approach to demonstrate and guide child through play in learning specific spatial concepts. Much will come through experimentation in play, especially with other children, but the child will develop more and sharper concepts of spatial organization and a stronger, richer interest in block building if he/she is guided to use, recognize, and talk about the characteristics and differences between the following sample of specific spatial concepts: Placing blocks together Intervals: Leaving a space (and later a series of spaces) between blocks Balance Bridges with a single block Tunnels Stairs Cantilevers (blocks that extend out from the top of another; two extending blocks can meet to form a bridge/tunnel) Enclosure (partial and total): two and three dimensional—thus rooms Windows and doors	14–30

II. GROUP STRUCTURES (cont.)

Concepts and Rules	Materials	How to Teach	Age to Begin (Mos.)
		Floors and ceilings Layers and levels Right, acute, and oblique angles; curves Roadways (including changes in direction) Ramps Columns (to hold up a floor) Porches Networks and systems (see section II.C.)	14–30
Part-whole Relations (of spatially localized sets of discrete objects) Groups of objects consist of more than one object, all of which form part of the entire group.	All types of objects; pictures and diagrams of objects clustered to illustrate different part-whole arrangements.	Essentially the same general approach, without complex spatial organization tasks demanded in learning the main body of spatial grouping concepts. Use *discrimination-recognition* (analysis) and *take apart-put together* (integration) activities as in teaching part-whole relations with whole objects and materials (continuous matter)—(see Section I.C.3.), except in this case playing with collections of objects in clusters (making the manipulations easier and quicker and without the definite form object structures have). Begin teaching part-whole relations with a few, identical objects (e.g., four or five cubes or identical toy cars), gradually increasing the objects in number (to about twenty) and variety. The following is a sample of terms to be used with corresponding part-whole arrangements:	18–24

Part	*Whole*
Parts	All, the group (set)
Some, any	The whole group (set)
A few, several	
A lot, lots	
Many	

More precise and detailed teaching of part-whole and other mathematical concepts is developed in Section III.

continued

II. GROUP STRUCTURES (cont.)

B. DESIGNS AND PATTERNS (AESTHETIC STRUCTURES)

> *Objects can be organized according to aesthetic principles.*

Concepts and Rules	Materials	How to Teach	Age to Begin (Mos.)
General			
Objects can be organized according to aesthetic principles for patterning form and color (e.g., order, rhythm, symmetry, balance, composition, etc.) that lend interest and beauty	A wide variety of two and three dimensional, free form (plastic art) and modular (construction) materials, such as for: —drawing, painting, collage, charcoal (two dimensional, free form) —sculpting, sand molding, carving (three dimensional, free form) —mosaics, design puzzles (two dimensional, modular) —construction blocks, bricks, interlocking construction materials (three dimensional, modular)	The general approach aims at developing children's awareness of aesthetic principles of design in order to appreciate and create interesting and appealing designs, through: 1. Fostering play with open-ended materials—modular and free form. 2. Encouraging children to experiment with design principles, aided by discussing form, color, and structural organization rules of shaping and building in various media. 3. Exposing children to a wide variety of models of designs in various media, comparing "good" and "bad" examples of various principles. 4. Guiding children in specific techniques and rules of design. Operations are all essentially analyzing and synthesizing (looking at elements and parts and interrelating and putting them together) —some on the basis of models and some from memory and imagination. Sequencing moves from the simplest two- and three-part structures with little order to complicated patterns and complex systems or organizations (e.g., block structures, drawings and sculptures with elaborate designs, scenes, and figures), sometimes including one or more subsystems (e.g., wings of buildings, elaborations of sections of larger compositions, complex parts of total scenes, etc.)	 6–12 18–24 24–30 24–30

II. GROUP STRUCTURES (cont.)

C. STRUCTURAL-FUNCTIONAL GROUPS
AND ORGANIZATIONS [a]

> *Objects interrelated to do things.*

Concepts and Rules	Materials	How to Teach	Age to Begin (Mos.)
General			
Objects and materials can be put together in different ways (type of connection); and shaped or constructed to perform particular functions (types of action).	All kinds of multipart objects or structures whose connections between parts and functional features are readily visible and easy to understand (e.g., tools, utensils, furniture, vehicles, simple machines, etc.) Pictures, drawings and diagrams that display connections and features clearly and selectively.	General model of language coordinated, sensory motor play learning activities, used as follows: 1. Identifying, comparing, and labeling the physical characteristics (mechanisms) by which the components of structural-functional groups of many types interconnect, interact, and are organized. 2. Dismantling and assembling simple structures of all kinds according to the child's skill development (analytic and synthesizing operations). 3. Pictures, drawings and diagrams, when available in clear form, are useful to supplement and clarify concepts first acquired through the more active manipulation of materials. Since pictures are often smaller and more manipulable than the objects themselves, pictures may lend themselves to easy manipulative play for discrimination learning activities (i.e., "Which is the picture of the machine connected by bolts?").	24–48
There are major types or areas of	Sample materials drawn from the	Teach at each of the *three levels of complexity* listed below *in order*, drawing	

---

[a] Extension of structural-functional relations from object recognition (Section I.B.) to more complex, multifaceted objects and organizations.

continued

II. GROUP STRUCTURES (cont.)

Concepts and Rules	Materials	How to Teach			Age to Begin (Mos.)
knowledge (levels of organization in each of which structural-functional relations operate at increasing levels of complexity	major areas of knowledge for each of the three successive levels of complexity	*simple* examples from the major areas of knowledge indicated:			24–48
		Linear (Chains)	*Area (Networks)*	*Three Dimensions (Systems)*	
		(one track structural-functional interactions) (12–18 months)	(two dimensional structural-functional interaction) (24–36 months)	(structures with multiple interacting parts and purposes) (36–48 months)	
Physical-Mechanical					
	Tools	*Single purpose tools:* hammer, screw driver, saw, pliers	*Dual purpose tools:* vice and saw; clamps and glue; nut, bolt, and wrench	Machines (e.g., vacuum cleaners) Engines (including vehicles with engines)	
	Complex objects	*Connecting mechanisms:* linking (chains), hooking, coupling (trains, car-trailer); braiding, tying, nailing, screwing	*Covering materials:* Weaving (rugs, cloth) nailing (floors) tying (nets)	*Three way combinatory structures* clothes, houses, furniture, vehicles	
Electro-Chemical					
	Electrical processes Chemical processes	*Simple electrical reactions* spark, lightning *Simple chemical reactions* burning, rotting	Electrical circuit (e.g., battery-bell) Electro-chemical circuits (e.g., batteries—with top or side open)	Electric motor Biochemical systems (e.g., digestion; breathing)	

II. GROUP STRUCTURES (cont.)

Concepts and Rules	Materials	How to Teach		Age to Begin (Mos.)
Biological				
	Plants and Animals	*Simple processes:* eating, eliminating, or doing single acts	*Ecological networks:*	Individual plant systems Individual animal systems (each composed of several interrelated systems for life support, development, and procreation)

Ecological networks:

predators (e.g., wolf, coyote) — carbon monoxide, fertilizer, oxygen → plants

herd size | food

fertilizer, carbon monoxide, food—oxygen

grazers (e.g., moose, deer)

Individual plant systems — 24–48

Concepts and Rules	Materials	How to Teach		
Social				
	Human, insect, bird, mammal: social groups	*Simple processes:* two person and two animal relations of sharing, helping, nurturing, communicating	*Social networks* three or more member groups cooperating on a common task or communicating	*Hierarchical groups and Organizations:* groups, institutions, and societies with leader-follower relations, division of labor and roles (e.g., human groups, ant colonies, beehives, bird flocks, etc.).

III. GROUP STRUCTURES—ABSTRACT: LOGICAL GROUPS AND ORGANIZATIONS

> **Objects can be grouped and organized on the basis of selected (abstracted) characteristics to form logical groups and organizations that transcend time and space.**

A. SERIAL ORDER (SERIATION)

> *Ordering objects quantitatively in a series according to abstracted dimensions of concrete and relational characteristics.*

Concepts and Rules	Materials	How to Teach	Age to Begin (Mos.)
General			
Objects can be placed in sequences (series) of increasing and decreasing quantity on dimensions of size, number, and other relational characteristics and concrete properties:	Selected sets of objects and materials that vary from low to high in value *only* on chosen characteristics.	Present all types of objects and materials in series, each scaled according to a chosen dimension (e.g., size, temperature, weight), using the same basic teaching strategy of language and action through play described for teaching object recognition (Section I.B.).	24–48
	A variety of sets of common objects and materials that vary from low to high on chosen characteristics *and* from few to many other irrelevant characteristics.	1. In this case, the demonstration-comparison activities naturally involve working with groups of objects, arranged in order on each dimension at various levels and degrees of difference along the scale.	
		2. Moreover, comparing activities (i.e., inquiring about differences—discriminating, and inquiring about similarities—matching) requires comparisons between at least two series for discriminating (e.g., "In which group are the toys arranged by how long they are?") and at least three series for matching (e.g., "Which of these two groups of toys is arranged by size, just like that group?"—pointing to a third group set slightly apart from the first two).	
	Artificial Materials		
	Many commercial (e.g., Montessori) and homemade materials can be expressly designed to point up	3. Sequencing should follow two basic paths:	

III. GROUP STRUCTURES—ABSTRACT (cont.)

Concepts and Rules	Materials	How to Teach	Age to Begin (Mos.)
	gradations in quantity.	a. Start with comparisons of two objects contrasted, for example, in height, in a manner similar to that of recognizing objects by their material characteristics of shape, color, etc., (Section I.B.3). Gradually increase the number of items and fineness of differences between items compared for size in the series (i.e., 2, 3, 4, 5, etc.) as the child progresses. Be sure to inquire alternately between higher valued (e.g., "Which is/are taller?") and lower valued (e.g., "Which is/are shorter?") on each dimension compared. b. Begin with sets of objects to place in order that vary *only* on a selected dimension (e.g., brightness), so it stands out, but gradually introduce other objects that vary randomly in other irrelevant characteristics of color, shape, etc. Color coding variations (as in Cuisenaire rods and stacking toys) should *not* be used until the child has mastered the tasks with uniformly colored series). c. Begin the teaching of each graded series using one simple term consistently to describe the comparison (e.g., big-bigger and small-smaller, hot-cool, rough-smooth). Gradually add more exact terms as the child progresses (e.g., wide-narrow; fat-thin; hot-warm-cool). 4. The bulk of the comparison should be *direct* in these early stages, deferring instruction in formal or *indirect measurement* (e.g., using rulers, thermometers, scales, etc.) to a later period. Similarly, rules about *conservation*, which require reciprocal manipulation of opposing dimensions, should be deferred (Section III.C.).	24–48

continued

III. GROUP STRUCTURES—ABSTRACT (cont.)

Concepts and Rules	Materials	How to Teach	Age to Begin (Mos.)
On such *specific dimensions as:*			
1. *Size*			
(continuous substances) Objects can vary in size, regardless of their particular characteristics, in three ways:			
a. *Linear* Objects can vary in size in a single direction (dimension) of length, width, height, depth, etc.	Sets of graded materials (e.g., rods; sticks; unit blocks; pencils; tinker toy sticks; rulers; strips of paper or lengths of flat boards; Montessori rods; etc.), very similar (including uniformity in color) except for variation in one dimension. Miscellaneous graded sets of longish objects more or less similar except for length variations (e.g., dolls, pencils, miniature figures, Cuisenaire rods, multicolored paper). Miscellaneous bulky objects that can be arranged in a series accord-	Follows general approach. It is important to keep other dimensions constant in every series, changing *only* length, *or* width *or* height, throughout all comparisons. Other visual characteristics, like color, shape, and features should initially be identical, then gradually varied. Transparent containers and open pails can be filled with liquids (e.g., water, identically colored water, glasses of juice at snack time) to make direct comparisons of depth (ignoring volume). Changes in width, length, and height can be demonstrated alternately with many of the same materials, simply by changing the orientation of the series as it is placed before the child: longways = length; sideways = width; on end = height. Vary the language term employed according to the orientation, but *begin first with long-short*, bringing in wide-narrow, tall-short, etc., gradually.	24–36

III. GROUP STRUCTURES—ABSTRACT (cont.)

Concepts and Rules	Materials	How to Teach	Age to Begin (Mos.)
	ing to differences in *just one dimension* (i.e., length, width, or height).		24–42
	Sets of tall and slender, *identical* transparent bottles, glasses, and jars or wide, open jars and pails.		
b. *Area* Objects can vary in size in two directions (dimensions), simultaneously e.g., in length *and* width (or height).	Sets of *identical* materials graded in two dimensions (e.g., flat boards, identically colored paper, Montessori materials, etc.). Miscellaneous sets of *similar* objects, which can be graded in *only* two dimensions (e.g., boxes, multicolored paper, and flat boards). *Dissimilar* objects that can be placed in graded series in *only* two ways. (Use above objects in various combinations.)	Follows general approach. It is important to vary no more than two dimensions at a time, holding the third constant in every comparison, and again other characteristics should initially be identical, then gradually varied. Thus, boards and boxes are placed in pairs (then in series) according to variations in width and length (but not thickness or height), first alternately, then in combination—but always *in the same direction* to increase or decrease the area. Opposite dimensional shifts are better brought in later to teach conservation (see Section III.C.). Later, alternate, then simultaneous variations in thickness (or height) in combination with width *or* length—but not both—may be played with to show area variations on the vertical plane. Switch language terms accordingly, but *begin with big-little* for all comparisons, using large-small and later (after a few weeks or months of consistent weekly experience, according to progress) pointing out that changes occur in both *length* and *width*.	24–42
c. *Volume* Objects can vary in size in three	Sets of *identical* materials graded systematically in	Follows general model, but focus is on volume with various combinations of dimensions varied simultaneously, first with	24–42

continued

III. GROUP STRUCTURES—ABSTRACT (cont.)

Concepts and Rules	Materials	How to Teach	Age to Begin (Mos.)
directions (dimensions) simultaneously, i.e., length, width *and* height.	three dimensions (e.g., stacking cups, boxes, rings; graded cubes, boxes, dolls, etc.). Sets of *similar* three-way graded materials (e.g., dolls, cars, multi-colored blocks, boxes, jars, toy cars, and figures.) Sets of *dissimilar* materials that can be graded in three ways (use combinations of above materials). Transparent or wide-mouth (squarish and cylindrical) containers that vary in two or three dimensions.	identical, then similar and dissimilar materials. Boxes, blocks, boards, dolls, and transparent or wide-mouth containers (both squarish and cylindrical) can vary in one (e.g., depth), two (e.g., width and length or length and height), or three dimensions, presented so that the dimensions increase (or decrease) consistently in the same direction. Begin by varying dimensions singly in turn in order to isolate the effects on volume, then varying two and finally three —being sure that variations always occur *in the same direction* to increase or decrease volume. The more complex problem of opposite dimensional shifts leads to conservation, which should follow this level (see Section III.C.). Use labels appropriately, but begin simply with big-small, then bigger-smaller. Begin indicating and labeling the changes in the separate dimensions (first two, then three) only after a few months of systematic experience with changes with similar and dissimilar materials.	24–42
2. *Number* (discontinuous substances or discrete objects). Sets of objects can vary in number, regardless of their particular characteristics.	A wide assortment of *identical* (e.g., pennies, single color cubes, poker chips), *similar* (e.g., dolls, miniature vehicles) and *dissimilar* (i.e., combinations) sets of mainly small objects and materials.	Follows general language-manipulation and play model for teaching. Like comparisons of physical quantity in size, but concerns comparisons of quantity of groups (sets) of objects rather than amount of material in a coherent object or substance. For this reason, comparisons are more complicated and abstract, and spacing between number sets in a series must be wide enough to make the sets stand out but narrow enough to make direct visual comparisons easy. It is also particularly helpful to teach number seriation through first using identical, then similar, and only finally dissimilar materials.	30–48

III. GROUP STRUCTURES—ABSTRACT (cont.)

Concepts and Rules	Materials	How to Teach	Age to Begin (Mos.)
		In addition to sequencing in terms of discriminating (pointing), identifying (naming), and matching sets by number, the order of difficulty for teaching should proceed in groups of two or three (and later larger) sets as follows:	30–48
		A. One versus two versus some indefinite quantity (lots, few, many, some) B. One versus two versus three C. Two versus three versus four D. and so on	
		It is preferable to teach comparisons of number sets (cardinality) initially without emphasizing counting (which points up ordinality). Counting at first tends to focus on the object he/she touches (i.e., one object) instead of the number he/she accumulates as he/she counts objects in a set (i.e., 1, 2, 3, . . .)	
		More complex operations with numbers (e.g., arithmetic operations, conservation) can be introduced as the child learns to seriate by numbers greater than three or four with similar materials. See section on conservation (III.C.).	
3. *Sound* a. *Volume* (intensity) Musical and other sounds can vary in loudness. b. *Pitch* (high-low) Musical and many other	Musical instruments and some noise-making objects that have sounds that can be varied widely or represent a graded series in volume, pitch, or tempo. (e.g., rows of identical bottles filled with water to different	Follows general model. Manipulation of musical and other sounds occurs sequentially through time, however, and thus increases demands, memory, and abstracting processes as noted in object recognition (Section I.B.). Thus the child's skill in comparing and matching sounds in series is likely to be slower to develop, except that the inherent appeal of musical patterns arouses compensating interest. For this reason make many comparisons through musical pieces, songs, and scale representation.	30–48

continued

III. GROUP STRUCTURES—ABSTRACT (cont.)

Concepts and Rules	Materials	How to Teach	Age to Begin (Mos.)
sounds can vary in pitch. c. *Duration* (short-long) d. *Tempo* (pace) Musical and other sound patterns can vary in the rate at which they occur (reciprocally related to duration).	levels or hollow bamboo of different lengths for illustrating pitch).	Teaching seriation of sound (order of increasing-decreasing loudness, pitch, duration, or rate) should continue from the activity of contrasting pairs of sound begun with recognizing material characteristics of objects, increasing the number in a series and adding the more difficult contrasts of tempo. Gradually vary the number in a series from two to three and more, going as far as the child can comfortably compare (about four or five). Teach only one serial pattern at a time, until the child has clearly mastered ordering of volume, pitch, duration, and tempo separately. Teaching musical sounds is of course closely linked to teaching music (appreciation, singing, and playing instruments) as an aesthetic experience.	30–48
4. *Light* (Brightness) Lights (and objects) vary in the amount of light they can emit.	Various types and brightness of light (as in I.B.3.). Select some lights whose intensity can be varied continuously and sets of lights graded in brightness. Sets of *similar* and *dissimilar* objects that vary in brightness.	Follows general model and continues brightness teaching started in object recognition activities (Section II.B.), moving now to series of three to five (or more) degrees of brightness, progressing as the child learns. At this point, begin teaching about light in two *forms*: 1. Differences in degrees of brightness of lights (e.g., flashlights, lamps, etc.). 2. Differences in degrees of brightness of almost any set of common objects (e.g., light, lighter—dark, darker). In both instances, the lights and the objects should be initially *similar*, especially in uniformity of color (both between objects and within the same object). Later introduce objects of gradually more contrasting color	30–48

III. GROUP STRUCTURES—ABSTRACT (cont.)

Concepts and Rules	Materials	How to Teach	Age to Begin (Mos.)
		shades and other features, although variations of color and other characteristics of objects must be limited or brightness differences become obscured.	30–48
5. *Temperature* Objects—including the air around us—vary in temperature (degrees of heat or cold)	All sorts of objects that show temperature changes with changing conditions, especially liquids, metals, rocks, and glass. Stoves and fire (on a limited basis).	Follows general model, also continuing temperature contrast teaching begun in object recognition activities (Section I.B.) and comparing three or more points of difference at different levels and degrees of difference. At this stage a distinction between *reflected heat* on ordinary objects (e.g., rocks from sun, heating water and food by the stove, etc.) and *heat sources* that generate heat (e.g., fire, electricity) can be made. The former are taught by handling in the usual manipulative play with language commentary (e.g., hot-warm, cool, cold, hotter, etc.); the latter, by feeling the radiated hot (or cold) air, outdoor and indoor temperature changes, and teaching about hazards, but avoid touching hot things (as described in Section I.B.). The main activity, however, is focused on acquiring serial order concepts of temperature differences using comparisons of objects systematically varied across a wide range of levels and degrees of difference. Metals, plates, jars of water, etc. deliberately heated or cooled to different temperatures are the best items for this purpose.	30–48
6. *Weight* Objects vary in weight (degrees of heaviness-lightness).	Many different objects and materials of small to moderate size, mostly those the child himself can lift. Sets of weight-graded objects of	Follows general model, starting with contrasting and matching pairs, since weight, like size, being more of a relational (abstract) comparison is perhaps better deferred until later infancy as scheduled in this plan. Extend the number of items compared (usually only to five or so), as the child progresses, moving from comparisons of objects of identical, then similar composi-	30–48

continued

III. GROUP STRUCTURES—ABSTRACT (cont.)

Concepts and Rules	Materials	How to Teach	Age to Begin (Mos.)
	identical, similar, and *varying composition* (to control density).	tion, so that weight will vary closely with size. Objects varying in composition (density) to the point that smaller objects (e.g., iron, lead, rocks) in a series weigh more than larger ones (e.g., balsa wood, ball of wool) should seldom be used until serial order concepts are well established with size differences and the child is ready to work with reciprocal changes in two dimensions as conservation requires (see Section III.C.).	30–48
7. *Taste and Smell Intensity* Many foods and other substances vary in strength of flavor and/or smell.	As many kinds of foods and substances to taste and smell as are conveniently available, which can be arranged in series to show obvious increasing-decreasing differences in strength of a selected taste and/or smell.	Follows general model, building on the object recognition and paired comparison activities of early infancy (see Section I.B.). Because substances are easier to identify when tasted (or smelled) in succession, rather than simultaneously, serial order learning in taste is similar in abstraction to ordering sounds. But also, like musical sounds, the enjoyment of food provides a strong interest basis for learning. Stick first to relatively *pure* substances in teaching taste/smell seriation, that is sets of identical foods that vary predominantly in one characteristic, salt, sour, sweet, burned, chocolate, etc., in order that differences in quantity (strength) along a single dimension can be grasped. Different kinds of foods (e.g., types of vegetables) can gradually be introduced as long as the amount of difference in "sourness" (or some other single dimension) remains obvious. Later, variations along two or more dimensions can be presented (but not usefully in terms of conservation—see Section III.C.).	30–48

III. GROUP STRUCTURES—ABSTRACT (cont.)

B. LOGICAL CLASSIFICATION

> *Grouping objects and materials abstractly according to selected. characteristics.*

Concepts and Rules	Materials	How to Teach	Age to Begin (Mos.)
General			

General

Objects and materials can be sorted into abstract groups (classes or sets), not necessarily sharing a common physical space or setting:

1. On the basis of different *types of distinguishing characteristics* (criteria); (see Table 1–1)

and

2. At many *levels of complexity* (number of classes and hierarchical levels) (see Table 1–1)

Materials

Various examples of objects and materials representing the categories of defining characteristics listed across the top of Table 1–1 and in previous guide sections as follows:

1. *Simple objects to illustrate:*

a. *Features-functions* (see Section I.B.)

b. *Material Characteristics* (see Section I.B.)

c. *Dimensions* (see Section III.A.)

2. *Multipart Objects and Structures to Illustrate:*

a. *Structural-Functional Relations* (see Section II.C.)

(1) Chain functional relations

How to Teach

Because the rules for organizing logical classes are abstract and complex, they must be taught through a series of increasingly complex steps over a period of several years. The most advanced levels can be traced to relatively simple selective sorting operations, easily started with older infants.

The steps for teaching classification can be organized as in the accompanying *sequence* (see Table 1–1).

Note that the order of difficulty proceeds roughly *both* from left to right across each row, according to the number and intricacy of defining characteristics, and vertically down each column according to the number of groups and levels.

Ages specified are estimates and frequently overlap because levels overlap in difficulty and children and programs may vary widely in rates of progression.

There are several *key rules* to teach children how to classify:

1. That objects can have *similar* characteristics;
2. That selected, *similar* characteristics define the group (class)—Table 1–1;
3. That unrelated, nondefining characteristics must be ignored;
4. That *all* the objects (available) with similar characteristics must be included in the group (class inclusion);
5. That *no* objects without the selected characteristics should be included (class exclusion).

Age to Begin (Mos.)

8–60
(see Table 1–1)

continued

TABLE 1-1 *Suggested Order of Steps and Starting Ages (10–60 Months) for Teaching Logical Classification*

Number of Levels in Hierarchy	Number of Groups (Classes) on Bottom Level	Simple Defining Characteristics		Multiple (3+) Defining Characteristic Types of Groups			
		Features Functions (see I.B.) (e.g., blade-cut) / Material Characteristics (see I.B.) (e.g., color, shape) — *Single Distinguishing Characteristic*	Dimensions (see III.A.) (e.g., size, brightness) — *Two Distinguishing Characteristics*	Structural-Functional Relations (see II.C.) — Functional Chain Relations (e.g., knife: handle, blade; fishing rod: handle, reel, line, hook, bait)	Networks (e.g., ecological relations, peer groups)	Systems (e.g., machines, social organizations)	Designs (see II.C.) (color-form aesthetic patterns)
Single (all groups on same level)	**One** A single group with distinguishing feature(s) versus Everything else undefined	10–12	12–18	18–24	24–36	18–30	18–30
	Two Two groups each with 1+ different distinguishing characteristics versus Everything else undefined	12–18	18–30	18–30	24–36	24–36	24–36
	Multi Groups (3+) Three (or more) groups defined versus Everything else undefined	18–30	24–36	30–42	36–48	36–48	36–48

Two Levels [a]
e.g.,:

    Dishes

Cups   Plates

Multi Levels (3+) [a]

Eating Equip. (tools)

Dishes   Utensils

Cups Plates Forks Spoons

18–30	24–36	30–48	36–48	36–48	36–48
30–48	36–48	36–48	36–60	36–60	36–60

[a] Each time a new level is added, children should first be given extensive experience with only two groups in each class, before providing examples with three or more groups.

41

III. GROUP STRUCTURES—ABSTRACT (cont.)

Concepts and Rules	Materials	How to Teach	Age to Begin (Mos.)
	(2) Networks (3) Systems	These need to be repeatedly demonstrated at each successive level.	8–60 (see Table 1–1)
	b. *Art Designs and Compositions* (more or less abstract) (see Section II.B.). *Artificial Materials* Homemade and commercial materials can be or are designed to selectively differ by precise numbers and types of distinguishing characteristics resembling the above simple and multistructure categories. The advantage of such materials is standardization and simplicity: the nature or number of confusing irrelevant characteristics can be completely controlled. As an example of the simplest level of 1.a., i.e., single class with one defining feature; two plastic, transparent cubes with	*Teaching methods* should follow the same basic approach outlined earlier for teaching object recognition (see Section I.B.), using language-guided, sensory motor play activities. Language is critically important to logical classification because abstract groups are difficult to define without the aid of symbols (language labels).	

III. GROUP STRUCTURES—ABSTRACT (cont.)

Concepts and Rules	Materials	How to Teach	Age to Begin (Mos.)
	a tiny red ball at the center.		8–60 (see Table 1–1)
	The other, irrelevant, features could consist of one or more blue balls, green cubes, bits of wire, etc., around the tiny red ball.		

C. CONSERVATION

> *Constancy of quantity.*

Concepts and Rules	Materials	How to Teach	Age to Begin (Mos.)
General			
Materials can undergo changes in external (perceptual) features through various changes back and forth (reversibility) in shape or arrangement without gaining or losing in the amount (quantity) of material.	All kinds of materials that can easily be altered in arrangement or shape, according to the nature of the material, without changing quantity.	Follows general approach to teaching object recognition (see I.B.) and especially serial order (see III.A.). Teaching conservation is a direct outgrowth of the comparisons of series of objects in terms of number, length, size, weight, and volume described in Section III.A. Understanding conservation, however, or the invariance of quantity, requires teaching the child several critical rules: 1. *Identity* (invariance): that the material remains unchanged (invariant) in amount (quantity), despite superficial (perceptual) changes in shape or arrangement. 2. *Reversibility*: that changes in any direction can be reversed without changing quantity.	30–60

continued

III. GROUP STRUCTURES—ABSTRACT (cont.)

Concepts and Rules	Materials	How to Teach	Age to Begin (Mos.)
		3. *Compensation or reciprocity*: that changes in one perceptual aspect (e.g., dimension of length) in a substance must always be matched by an *equal and opposite* change of another aspect (e.g., dimension of width)—thus quantity remains constant.	30–60
		4. *Equivalence*: that two forms (or sets) of material, originally established as equivalent (or smaller or larger) in quantity, remain equal (or smaller or larger) in quantity, despite superficial changes.	
		The application of these rules to the various types of conservation is indicated below:	
Specific Types: Number (discontinuous quantity) The number of objects in a set remains the same regardless of how they are moved or arranged.	A number of sets of small identical, similar, and dissimilar objects. (See III.A.) Food, using many discrete objects (e.g., peas, beans, raisins).	Procedures to teach conservation rules in the number area involve: 1. Changing the position and arrangement of sets of objects placed in clusters, using first identical, then similar, and eventually dissimilar materials, gradually increasing the numbers in the sets (from one to two to three . . . etc.), to indicate irrelevance of changes to number. 2. Showing how increases (or decreases) in *density* (closeness) of objects are matched by corresponding decreases (or increases) in *area* (or length, for sets placed in a row). 3. Matching two sets of objects (again, from identical to dissimilar) in parallel rows to teach one-to-one correspondence (equivalence), using sets of identical and different numbers and changing positions and arrangements from and back to the original positions. 4. Adding and subtracting objects (one, two, three, etc.) from single and parallel sets to show how *real* changes in number	30–48

III. GROUP STRUCTURES—ABSTRACT (cont.)

Concepts and Rules	Materials	How to Teach	Age to Begin (*Mos.*)
		occur (and can be restored) as opposed to irrelevant changes in position that affect density and area (or length), but not number.	30–48
Length The length of an object stays the same regardless of how it is moved or arranged.	A number of sets of identical, similar, and dis- similar long objects of different widths (see III.A.). Sets of take apart-put together rods, unit blocks, etc., that can be assembled and dismantled in different lengths. Food in long strips (e.g., celery, string beans, carrot strips, etc.).	Procedures to teach conservation rules, applied to length include: 1. Making direct comparisons between, (two or more) sticks (and various longish objects of different widths), placed parallel and moved back and forth to show how changes in position do not affect length. 2. Showing how "increases" (or decreases) in length at one end, which are due merely to changes in position, must be matched by equivalent "decreases" (or increases) in length at the other end. 3. Using unit blocks (or take-apart rods) to add and subtract sections of various lengths to show how *real* changes in length can occur (compared to relative changes due to positional shifts that only shorten (or lengthen) one end or the other, relative to a parallel stick); show how adding a section equal in length to a section sub- tracted (at either end) restores (reverses) the rod to the original length.	30–48
Substance (solid volume) The amount of material stays the same regardless of how you change its shape and structure.	Several types of malleable sub- stances, such as plasticene, pot- ter's clay, play dough, mashed foods (e.g., potatoes, squash), and wet mud or sand.	Procedures to teach conservation rules applied to substance include: 1. Changing the shape of pliable material (e.g., plasticene, clay) to show how such changes do not change the amount. 2. Showing how changes in shape in one way (e.g., increases or decreases in thick- ness) are matched by compensating changes in another way (e.g., decreases or increases in length) to keep quantity constant. 3. Comparing two pieces of plasticene, of equal and unequal amounts, to show how	30–48

continued

III. GROUP STRUCTURES—ABSTRACT (cont.)

Concepts and Rules	Materials	How to Teach	Age to Begin (Mos.)
		changes in shape in different ways from and to the original, do not change equality ("same") or inequality ("more-less") in quantity.	30–48
		4. Adding and subtracting differing amounts of plasticene, from single pieces (or two pieces for comparison), to show how *real* alterations of substance occur (and can be reversed-restored), as compared to changes in shape that do not affect the amount; show that if a piece removed from one side is added (or if an equivalent piece is replaced somewhere) to another side, the original amount is restored.	
Weight The weight of materials (or objects) remains the same regardless of changes in shape or structure.	Pliable substances like clay, plasticene, etc., and mashed foods (similar to conservation of substance).	Procedures to teach conservation rules for weight are *similar to those for teaching conservation of substance.* *The difference:* 1. Judgments of identity (no change in weight), equivalence, etc., are made through lifting materials (weighing objects by feel) or by a scale (to *test* differences more accurately), instead of simply by visual scanning. Judgments are therefore more abstract and take longer to learn. 2. *But, like substances*, the manipulations of materials are those of shape that do not affect weight. Addition-subtraction is also similar.	36–60
Area (surface) The amount of space in a surface area remains the same regardless of its shape or the distribution of objects of total equivalent area filling the space.	Colored construction paper (and boards, cardboard, cookies, etc.) cut in pairs of differing shape but equal in area, together with smaller, standard unit	Procedures to teach conservation rules for area are: 1. Mainly through making comparisons of two (and later three) surface areas of different shape but equal in total area to show equivalence. Smaller unit cutouts whose combined total area equals either shaped area are alternately placed on the two areas in different arrangements to demonstrate equivalence (in the usual way	36–60

III. GROUP STRUCTURES—ABSTRACT (cont.)

Concepts and Rules	Materials	How to Teach	*Age to Begin (Mos.)*
	shapes (of cutout paper, cardboard, or blocks) which can be fitted into the larger areas in different combinations.	in play, alternately by the teacher and the child). The smaller unit shapes must be cut to a standard length and width in order to fit many different larger shapes, and must be some exact proportion of the length and width of both figures (modular). Draw attention to reciprocal changes in length and width by showing how more modules are used one way or the other. Only certain shape comparisons are feasible with fixed materials because of the impossibility of changing the shapes of the component objects to fit larger irregularly shaped areas. Thus only two basic shape comparisons are feasible:	36–60

a. Various comparisons of right-angle figures, varying in length and width (but always equal in area), from squares to long, thin rectangles. The unit modules that fit best are small cutout squares; for example, one inch (two and one-half centimeter) squares would fit easily into larger multi-inch squares and rectangles. Modular rectangles would be difficult to work with.

b. Various comparisons of, polygon figures (multisided angular figures), whose area can be *exactly* filled by different sized and shaped small triangles (and/or other small multisided figures). Nonright-angle figures are more difficult for preschoolers, however.

2. Making comparisons with unit materials between surfaces equal in shape but different in area to show real changes in area, i.e., which require different numbers of units to cover the area.

3. Adding and subtracting the smaller unit cutouts from the larger areas (each area separately and by comparison of different shapes), to show how areas can be built

continued

III. GROUP STRUCTURES—ABSTRACT (cont.)

Concepts and Rules	Materials	How to Teach	Age to Begin (Mos.)
		up of equal area components in different combinations. (This is a beginning of area measurement.) These operations can also show the effect of real changes in area, both with and without changing shape, depending on which component units are removed or added.	36–60
Volume (liquid) The amount of material in a container remains the same regardless of the shape of a container.	Water, milk, juices, artificially colored liquids and sand, and transparent containers in combinations of equal and different sizes and shape, but preferably proportionate in volume so relations are pointed up (e.g., one-quarter, one-half, and three-quarters full).	Procedures to teach rules for conservation of volume with liquid type materials consists of: 1. Pouring liquids (and sand) back and forth (reversibility) between pairs (and later sets) of containers equal in volume but differing in shape (e.g., tall and thin versus short and wide) to show equivalence. Draw attention to the principle of reciprocal changes in different dimensions. 2. Pouring the same amounts of liquid back and forth among containers that differ in both shape and volume to show that changes in shape make quantity look larger or smaller in volume. Again draw attention to reciprocal changes in dimensions. 3. Comparing the effects of pouring a given quantity of liquid into containers identical in shape but different in size, showing the constancy of a liquid quantity relative to real changes in container volume.	36–60

IV. PROCESSES (CHANGE) MEANS-END RELATIONS

> **Change is characteristic of all things.**

A. STRUCTURE OF CHANGE

> *Defining the organization and dimensions of change processes.*

Concepts and Rules	Materials	How to Teach	Age to Begin (Mos.)
General			
Processes of change may be defined in terms of a number of aspects or dimensions (causality, sequence, etc.), each of which can be identified in *several forms* of change (e.g., with and without alteration of materials) and in *different types or levels of natural processes* (e.g., mechanical, chemical, biological, and social):	All types of common objects and materials, according to the nature and aspect of change to be taught, including plants, animals, and people. Small, clearly structured objects and devices with which the child can try out the changes himself/herself or observe them easily, close at hand. Artificial materials and devices, either commercial or homemade (operating by buttons, levers, sliding doors, etc.). Drawings and pictures that illustrate clearly some particular aspect of change; draw-	The same general model of teaching concepts through demonstrating and participation in language, guided, sensory motor play (Section I.B.) is employed with certain modifications: 1. Processes are more elusive and abstract than most object recognition and spatial structural activities (Sections I and II), because processes involve movement and successive changes that disappear, unlike static objects and organizations. Many forms of change leave no visible record or leave outcomes with no evident connection to previous states of things (e.g., even simple movement of objects). 2. Nevertheless, processes are often hardly more abstract or complex than the abstract relations in quantitative series (seriation, Section III.A.) or logical classification (III.B.) and can be taught to young children by starting with simple examples, pacing, sequencing, and comparing in play as described for object recognition activities (Section I.B.). For example, the very first focus on change for the infant is movement—his own and the objects around him (see Section I.A.). Change is in fact built into many of the operations needed to demonstrate previous structural concepts, including movements to show object concepts, seriation, and grouping objects by defining characteristics (logical classification, Section III.B.).	0–60

continued

IV. PROCESSES (CHANGE) (cont.)

Concepts and Rules	Materials	How to Teach	Age to Begin (Mos.)
ings can simplify and rearrange parts to illustrate change, particularly the cause (means) and series of steps in change, sometimes better than the thing itself (e.g., a vacuum cleaner or other machine whose inner parts are ordinarily hidden).		3. The purpose of a separate program for teaching change is to develop a more systematic understanding of the means and ends rules of change.	0–42
Such diagrammatic types of drawings are made with complex coding rules, better for older preschoolers (ages three to five).		4. The particular procedures are described mainly in terms of common mechanical forms of change, the most meaningful form at the preschool level. 5. Because of the successive, disappearing quality of change processes, it is particularly important to: a. Repeat the necessary movements frequently in different ways and contexts to develop general understanding. b. Vary the speed and isolate significant features and steps in a process. c. Draw heavily from the actions and events in which the child is directly and familiarly involved (e.g., the physical and social routines of care and other activities revolving around the child's daily activities in day care, school, and at home).	

B. DIMENSIONS OF CHANGE

Concepts and Rules	Materials	How to Teach	Age to Begin (Mos.)
1. *Causality* Change is caused by objects or events (means) producing other objects or events (ends or effects).	Same	Teaching causality is centered on learning structural-functional relations, which begins with learning features and functions (Section I.B.) in object recognition activities but should more systematically: 1. Draw attention to and label *what* produces (originates) various changes, that is	12–24

IV. PROCESSES (CHANGE) (cont.)

Concepts and Rules	Materials	How to Teach	Age to Begin (Mos.)
		what instrument or tool (structural means), such as the feature of objects (e.g., hand of person, blade of knife, point of crayon).	12–24

2. Draw attention to and label *how* change occurs, that is, the form of the action (functional means) by which change occurs (e.g., throwing a ball, cutting a cake, heating water).

3. It is important to help the infant to gradually distinguish between the effects of her/his own actions and the *work of specific tools* and functions, sometimes operated by her/him, and sometimes worked by others, or by independent causes (e.g., fire, wind, gravity, growth, machines, etc.).

4. There are several *key rules* or steps to developing an understanding of causality; he/she must develop awareness:

a. That *change occurs*—simply drawing attention to movement is the first basis for learning causality.

b. That things (means) produce effects (ends)—hands and other objects used as tools to do things.

c. That particular objects have particular features (specific means) to perform specific actions or functions (specific ends)—the focus on structural-functional relations described in Items 1 and 2 above.

d. That a particular means must act directly and closely in space in particular ways to produce effects—show by trying out particular actions at different distances.

e. That effects are often produced independent of human action, but that human action often with the aid of particular tools

continued

IV. PROCESSES (CHANGE) (cont.)

Concepts and Rules	Materials	How to Teach	Age to Begin (Mos.)
		can produce many different effects—Item 3 above.	12–24
		f. That effort (energy) is required to produce change, either human or an environmental source—show for example that the *child* must push, pull, beat (batter to make cake); or that fire uses wood, a spring unwinds, an engine uses fuel, etc., to do various tasks.	
		g. That there are *alternative means* and *alternative ends* with the same means—by using different hands and objects to do the same things (e.g., pushing with either hand, marking with several crayons) and the same tools to do different actions (e.g., hand to push, pull, pick up, hammer, and different boxes to hold the same objects). This more complex and abstract level is essentially close to logical classification (III.B.) and involves seeking various examples of particular types of means and ends, at various levels of abstraction. It is important to show that there are specific types of structural-functional relations—by showing for example that balls cannot slide nor blocks roll or that hammers can't screw nor screw drivers hammer.	
2. Sequence Change is a process that runs through an ordered series of means and end events, because causes must precede effects or because two component tasks	Same	Draw attention to (and label) the order of events in a change process. First isolate single means-end connections (e.g., grasping with fingers), gradually showing—by breaking each process into a set of steps (pausing between each)—how most processes consist of a chain of means-end events, which nevertheless have a beginning, middle and end (e.g., to put a block in a box: reaching, grasping, lifting, moving hand over box, dropping block in box).	18–30

IV. PROCESSES (CHANGE) (cont.)

Concepts and Rules	Materials	How to Teach	Age to Begin (Mos.)
cannot be done simultaneously.		Show how some sequences can be changed, because they are *not* causally connected (e.g., putting on either shoe first) and others cannot, because a second event is dependent on a preceding one (e.g., putting on a shoe after a sock). Sequential processes are closely related to teaching seriation or differences in size, length, brightness, etc. (see III.A.), but more abstract because processes disappear.	18–30
3. *Speed (rate)* Processes occur at different rates (fast-slow) relative to one another and may change speed (accelerate-decelerate).	Same	Show how (and label) movements (e.g., the child's and teacher's vehicles, mobiles, swings) and tasks can be performed or changes occur naturally at different speeds (from slow to fast); and how they can occur at increasing or decreasing speeds. Show how the speed at which change occurs or at which we perform tasks (produce changes) is partly the result of how complicated or delicate they are or how many steps there are in a sequence. Set up two tasks or movements side by side so the child can compare rates and changes in rates and try those he/she is capable of himself/herself. Speed and time are also both aspects of processes that lend themselves to *encouraging cooperation* in tasks, showing how tasks such as picking up toys, building block structures, or preparing means get done faster when two people work on tasks.	12–24
4. *Time (duration)* Processes last a certain period, because they occur in succes-	Same	The child's sense of time evolves through three phases: 1. *Need time.* The cycle of the rise and fall of inner needs of hunger, thirst, elimination, and (as the infant gets socialized) his/her pattern of needs for comfort, security, and	0–24 0–6

continued

IV. PROCESSES (CHANGE) (cont.)

Concepts and Rules	Materials	How to Teach	Age to Begin (Mos.)
sion, rather than all at once; different processes take different amounts of time, because they contain more events in a sequence and/or proceed at different rates.		stimulation. An immediate, noncomparative sense of time.	0–6

2. Activity Time. The cycle of daily routines and experiences the infant encounters in care and other activities shapes a wide sense of time, which builds on need time but, incorporates a more realistic sense of sequential process time, the time it takes to perform different tasks and activities. Comparisons between event cycles evolve.   0–6

Activities for teaching time at this level consist of:

a. Providing a balance between consistency and variation in caregiving routines and activities to develop a sense of predictability for events that mark the passage of time in activities, thus channeling the cycle of his/her needs to activity schedules. Too little consistency moves toward the unpredictability of chaos and impedes the development of activity time. Too rigid scheduling develops a rigid time sense that will not match the pattern of many processes of adult daily life.

b. Showing how movements and tasks vary in the time they take as a result of their complexity, the number of events in a series, the fragility of materials, or simply because of the different speeds at which they occur.

3. Objective Time. Conceptualizing time in an exact way is an outgrowth of the child's experiences from activity time, but requires the addition of measurement (chronological and calendar time), and an expanded knowledge of personal and societal life and historical events, which take some   18–24

IV. PROCESSES (CHANGE) (cont.)

Concepts and Rules	Materials	How to Teach	Age to Begin (Mos.)
		years of developmental education to acquire. The child should be exposed to concepts of both indefinite and definite concepts of time like the following:	18–24

Indefinite

Past: ago (a little while _____, a long time _____, a few minutes, hours, days, etc.,) was, did, earlier, yesterday, last week, month, etc.

Present: now, the present is, going on, is _____ing today, this minute, hour, week, etc. this morning, afternoon.

Future: soon, a long time from now, in a few minutes, hours, days, etc. will, shall, later, tomorrow, next week, month, etc.

Definite

Application of *exact labels* of chronological and calendar time systems:

Hours, minutes, seconds
Days of week
Months and dates of month
Seasons
Years and historical dates

Note that early and late are related to points of time in a sequence.

continued

IV. PROCESSES (CHANGE) (cont.)

C. FORMS AND TYPES (LEVELS) OF CHANGE

> *Change occurs in different forms and at different levels of organization of the natural world*

Concepts and Rules	Materials	How to Teach	Age to Begin (Mos.)
General			
Changes occur in several *forms* and in several types or *levels* of organization of natural processes (see Table 1–2)	Same; samples selected according to the *forms* and *levels* of complexity needed as illustrated in Table 1–2.	Follows the general model and set of guidelines described above (IV.A.). Examples of each of the *forms of change* (listed vertically in the left-hand column of Table 1–2) can be found for each of the different *types of natural processes* (listed across the top of Table 1–2), as illustrated in the appropriate boxes. The forms of change refer generally to the outcome, that is, whether or what kind of change occurs to the form of the material in a process. The types of natural processes refer to the different ways in which the physical world is organized, ranging from the simplest mechanical to the most complex processes of social organizations. They are often viewed as *levels* of organization because each successive process is constructed in terms of all preceding types. For each of the examples of interactions between forms and types, it is useful to analyze the processes in terms of the various dimensions, causality, sequence, etc. (See Section IV.B.). It will be noted that there is no clear age progression indicated for learning about either the forms of change or types of change. Much depends on whether simple and clear examples can be found; other examples may well permit the child to grasp the various concepts—or at least to begin teaching elements of the processes—earlier than the suggested age ranges.	6–42

TABLE 1–2. *Examples of and Suggested Ages (Months) to Begin Teaching Forms of Change at Each Major Level of Natural Processes.*

Types (Levels) of Organization of Natural Processes

Forms of Change Processes	Mechanical (physical)	Chemical (including omagnetic)	Biological	Social (including psychological and economic)
Movement Action-interaction	6-12 pushing, pulling, rolling bouncing two balls together	24–30 shaking or stirring chemical liquids, magnets, electricity	24–30 Swallowing, digestion, elimination, blood circulation (need good drawings)	6-12 movements of people, animals, and plants
Alteration Reorganization (rearrangement or replacement of parts)	12–18 rearranging box contents, furniture, block structure replacing a nut on a bolt	24–30 changing from liquids to solids (e.g., freezing water) or gas (steam)	24–30 pruning trees (which grow substitute branches) removing a starfish prong (which regenerates) cutting hair, fingernails	24–30 changing children or social (e.g., work or play) roles in a play group

TABLE 1-2. (continued)

Forms of Change Processes	Mechanical (physical)	Chemical (including electromagnetic)	Biological	Social (including psychological and economic)
Modification (addition or subtraction of parts without gain or loss of function)	18–24 removing or adding a nonessential decoration or part (e.g., piece of an eraser, a minor bolt in a car)	24–30 slight changes in temperature	24–42 removing tonsils or appendix small cuts to plants, animals, or people cutting hair, fingernails	24–42 adding or removing one or two children, minor roles, rules, or tasks
Development (gain in complexity of structure and function)	18–30 building modular structures (blocks) creating art forms building things (e.g., houses, machines)	36–42 making water from hydrogen and oxygen (H_2O) making an acid	24–42 growth of plants and animals from infancy developmental metamorphosis (e.g, eggs hatch)	24–42 organizing a play or work group and developing new roles, rules, or tasks
Destruction (damage to or loss of parts or function)	18–24 removal, damage, or destruction of any key features (e.g., ladle of spoon) or whole object	18–30 any burning (oxidation) or explosion (rapid oxidation)	24–42 handicapping cuts and injuries illness (temporary loss), aging, and death	30–42 breaking up a play or work group; eliminating major roles, rules, or tasks

2

Problem Solving Curriculum

Problem solving is at the root of all human activity. Every situation presents us with problems that we must solve in order to cope; that is, we have to figure out what to do and how to do it in any situation in order to get along or get what we want. We select a recipe, utensils, and ingredients to make a cake, or choose a design, tools, and lumber for making a table. The infant wants to find a way to retrieve an appealing toy on a shelf or to open a box with a captivating sound inside. The preschooler wants to find the right piece to fit a place in his/her puzzle or how to pile blocks to make a tall building. All life is a series of problems in how to cope.

In the course of solving such problems we are alternately learning and exercising skills and knowledge we already know. When we are highly familiar with a task, we apply our knowledge smoothly and there is of course little to learn. But in early childhood, almost every situation offers some new challenge to learn about, either in finding out about novel materials or trying out new possibilities with familiar materials. With a little guidance here and there and much active experimentation, the child works on problems naturally to develop his/her understanding and coping skills. The particular strength of a planned curriculum on problem solving is that it not only teaches the child general strategies of how to solve problems, but it also teaches her/him that problem solving is essential to the acquisition of knowledge or to accomplish anything at all. Thus selected experiences in learning tasks that focus on the processes and principles of solving problems, beyond the experience offered in an inquiry-oriented knowledge curriculum, are invaluable. It is particularly useful to provide experience in a wide range of practical, life situation problems to extend the child's coping competence.

Strategies for solving problems are one of the three basic aspects of mental processes. In any activity, we must have knowledge of the materials and how they work, we must be able to represent this knowledge in some shorthand form (code) such as language or pictures, and we must know how to work on problems, that is, figure out tasks and carry out activity. Each of these aspects of mental processing involves learning a different set of rules, but all must be used together in some way in order to perform a task. This chapter will outline a few of the main principles the child learns through problem-solving activities, followed by a series of practical problem-solving tasks to help the child become aware of these principles. Most of the tasks involve concrete, sensory motor actions normal to the little child's way of working out problems. But there are also guides for extending them into pictorial and verbal coding tasks in more abstract ways as the child develops.

PRINCIPLES OF PROBLEM SOLVING

INQUIRING, SEARCHING, AND EXPERIMENTATION

Solving problems begins and ends with asking questions, searching, and trying out how to work things. If children are always merely offered concepts to learn with the materials all fixed to work, or examples are laid out without any effort required, neither the nature of the concepts nor the processes of problem solving become mastered. At the extreme, the child learns a few examples by rote without learning the general characteristics that define the concepts; without these he/she will find it difficult to apply the concepts to new examples. Worse, he/she develops a passive approach to tasks, failing to understand the need for inquiring how and why, the need to search and *actively* experiment with problems to learn and find solutions.

The underlying key to an inquiry approach is the opportunity it offers the child to exercise his/her own mental processes. Always solving problems *for* the child stunts the child's independent mental development. He must learn to formulate and test his own ideas (hypothesis development and testing). The child must be actively engaged mentally, to manipulate the examples, ideas and relations in his own mind, through working on a problem to develop the full scope of his mind.

CAUSALITY: RELATING MEANS TO ENDS

The business of solving problems to carry out human activity is always a business of finding means to reach ends. Relating means to ends involves understanding causality, that is how certain things (means) make other things (ends) happen. Many events have complicated causes, of course, such as how plants grow or trucks are manufactured. But many events and things we do in everyday living have rather simple, direct causes children can learn to understand. Many simple tools, for example, have specific features (means) that perform particular functions (ends), as in the illustration of the broom and dustpan. And it is this specificity of function that particularly designed features perform which is at the core of understanding how events are caused, and thus how to solve problems. All problems are, in other words, composed of structural-functional relations that must be figured out to carry out a desired task.

Problems for children need not be restricted to tasks using special tools, of course. Although these are useful, fun, and listed as examples in the curriculum, many useful experiences in problem solving come through learning how to apply ordinary objects to different purposes. In this manner the child becomes more intellectually adaptive and creative in his/her daily encounters with life's problems. But in any case, the heart of the matter is learning to select useful means (particular structural mechanisms) to carry out (cause) desired goals (functions).

The natural course of development for infants is first to observe that things happen (e.g., movement) without any thought that something must make it happen. Soon they begin to see that certain things happen together. Through their activity they come to see that they can bring about events on their own, without quite realizing how. Next they learn that particular means are needed to produce particular ends (e.g., a rattle, but not a ball, will make a noise when shaken), which leads them to an expanding awareness of the general idea of independent causation. But they also eventually realize that various means offering the same or similar features can perform the same or similar functions. In this way they gradually learn to multiply their powers of control over events, as well as awareness of what they can and cannot do, processes greatly aided by guided experience in problem solving.

ALTERNATIVES

Experimentation with alternatives is thus central to developing awareness of causality and efficiency in problem solving. Fortunately, it is in the nature of problems and problem solving that there are alternatives. There are first the relevant elements and relations in a task, as opposed to all the background materials that have no value for the problem at hand. More important, there are usually different materials that can be used to accomplish the same purpose or at least they can be put together in a different order or different way. Either of two red crayons will make a red drawing, two long blocks will both bridge the same distance, and although each jigsaw piece fits only one space, the order of inserting them can often be varied. At the infant level, either hand will frequently perform the same action and one can approach a task from different angles. At more advanced levels, experience in problem solving teaches the child that several different means can be used to accomplish the same goal, such as reaching something on a shelf by piling blocks, positioning a chair, climbing on a nearby table, reaching with a long pole, or even asking a taller child or a teacher to reach for it. Goals themselves can be varied. Either a cookie or a piece of cake is a sweet that will please, and both puzzles and form boards are spatial matching problems. Of course, goals themselves are also means to still other ends, e.g., sweets satisfy a certain kind of appetite and working puzzle problems give pleasure and knowledge of spatial concepts.

ANALYZING AND SYNTHESIZING

Of all the rules for problem solving, learning to see parts and relations are among the most vital. As we have observed, every situation has many elements, of which only certain ones are important to a problem. The elements relevant to a problem, moreover, must be interrelated in such a manner that the problem is efficiently solved. From all the items in a kitchen, one chooses the broom and dustpan to sweep the floor, not, for example, a towel or a dish. Each of the selected objects, such as the broom and the dustpan, moreover, has particular features that must be employed in specific ways and the objects used together in an integrated manner to work. The same process of searching for relevant elements and features and how they can be interrelated is characteristic of all problem solving, whether it is for household tasks, manufacturing goods, or fitting pieces of a puzzle together.

COMPLEXITY: INFERENCING, ABSTRACTION, AND SEQUENCING

Offering a task for a child to carry out independently, with only limited guidance, creates a demand to think. It engages and develops mental processes, as was noted, through the inquiry and experimentation that is built into the processes of solving problems. The child is forced to make his/her own inferences (hypotheses) about how things could work. But these processes of abstracting the essential relations of means to ends in a task are quite limited if the elements of a task are always placed closely together in convenient relation to one another. To extend the child's mental powers it is necessary to pose problems in which he/she must infer what is needed and how to put together the elements to solve the problem. If everything needed is immediately visible and closely related, the analyzing and synthesizing of means and ends requires only very direct, sometimes almost rote, comparisons, with little call for mental abstracting of general principles.

There are several techniques for extending the abstractness and complexity of problems, all of which can probably be used with benefit as the child progresses. The first technique is simply to move the needed tools further from the goals, requiring the child to search over longer distances and wider areas. A second is to increase the number of parts (e.g., puzzle) or number of tools or steps needed to reach a goal (contingency chain). Opening a series of increasingly smaller boxes (e.g., nesting boxes or dolls) placed successively inside one another, piling several boxes to reach a high shelf, navigating a maze, or even making a cake with several ingredients or a wooden toy requiring measuring, sawing, gluing, screwing, and nailing are several such examples. A third technique is to present the needed means or tools in the midst of a clutter of other irrelevant objects. For example, if the task were to cross a narrow stream of water, several boards could be placed on the bank, only one of which is long enough to span the stream, and in addition other irrelevant objects, like boxes, tubs, blocks, tricycles, and rocks could be placed at hand. A fourth is to partially obscure the clues (cues), as in picking out the right block to fit into a block structure, choosing by touch alone among several different sized blocks in a paper bag. A fifth is by working with abstract codes. An example might consist of asking a child to choose a workable tool to perform a task through pictures, then bringing out a real example of the tool she chose for herself to see if it solves the problem. Copying pictured models of block buildings, rather than three dimensional models, is a variation of this technique. But the task can be made even more abstract by using language, asking the child whether she needs a round-ish or longish tool to reach a distant toy, for example. All of these and many other variations have in common the requirement of placing more demands on the child to search for and put things together in her head. She must make inferences on the basis of general rules, not literal forms, thus developing cognitive abilities more adaptively and creatively.

At the same time, the complexity of demands placed on children with this movement toward abstraction cannot be presented all at once or in just any order. It is a matter of gradualism, starting with the most obvious and simple forms of tasks, such as the infant reaching for an interesting toy in a box right in front of him, and moving eventually to finding the toy in a remote corner on the basis of verbal clues. The level of complexity or difficulty at which one brings the child into a sequence depends on what he already knows and how mentally developed he is in his motivations for working on problems. In general, the younger the infant, the simpler and more concrete the tasks, and the more slowly one moves to more abstract and complicated problems with many parts. But many older children cannot undertake difficult problems either; for various reasons, such as lack of prior stimulation or inconsistent encouragement in working on problems, they cannot understand or persist. It is not, however, necessary to set up a series of tasks that vary rigidly in complexity, one step at a time. It is better to move ahead by levels, that is, for example, presenting a variety of tasks during a period, all having more or less the same number of parts or missing cues. But one can also move back and forth, presenting a somewhat advanced problem now and then, while sticking to an easier level most of the time.

SAMPLE PROBLEM SOLVING SEQUENCES

In the sample series of problem tasks presented below, most of the tasks follow a simple form, demanding discovery of effective means to accomplish some desired end. A few of the problems, in particular barrier-detour tasks, are specifically designed to provide experience in overcoming obstacles. But all problems in fact present obstacles in some form, in the sense that discovering the right means and how to employ them always demands effort and skill, and thus builds obstacles into the very process of solving the problem. Using means and overcoming obstacles are simply two different ways of stating the process of finding solutions to problems.

Because most of the problems are set in the form of sensory motor tasks, concepts of spatial relations and the nature of objects (e.g., object permanence) and how they work are central to the learning involved. The tasks and sequences are designed to foster the child's understanding of various spatial concepts of size, shape, movement, position, and other relational concepts, as well as those of means and ends, causality, inferencing, and analyzing and synthesizing as described above.

For each type of problem solving sequence (e.g., object retrieval, tool using) the general form of the problem is defined across the first row at the top of each section, and the different difficulty levels are outlined in successive rows below. It should be noted that the ages indicated are merely suggested as age ranges during which children can probably benefit most from experience in the defined tasks. Broad ranges of this sort are essential, because each child's readiness depends so much on how much his/her skill and interest have already been developed through prior experience. The ranges listed for the successive age levels also overlap considerably, since the difficulty of the tasks overlap. As in many forms of learning, differences between concept levels are not absolute and the child needs to work back and forth between them to some degree. This arrangement tends to alternately challenge and build up confidence and mastery, thus fostering the general strength of the child's intelligence. The levels are nevertheless useful for indicating how tasks vary in complexity and also for suggesting the complexity of the level at which the child would be expected to learn most readily. Obviously, the task of instruction must be approached flexibly, diagnosing competence by initially offering problems at several different levels to find out just where to spend most of the time until the child is ready to move on to a more advanced level. The problem sequences themselves (e.g., barrier problems, tool using) may be introduced in any order and used alternately as seems useful.

The business of diagnosing each child's competence and determining when he/she is ready to move on is helped by the manner in which the problem tasks are described. Thus the description of the tasks at each level are divided into two columns, the first describes the main form of the learning task (next to last column); and is followed by concept generalization tasks (last column) listing suggestions for how to vary the task in order to both encourage and measure the child's progress in acquiring broad concepts of the relevant problem solving principles. Once a child can solve several problems under different conditions with relative ease, it is usually safe to assume the child is ready to spend most of his/her time at the next higher level. In any case there is nothing to prevent returning to problems at the simpler levels, when more experience seems indicated. Certain special *concepts* to be learned in each problem, beyond those general spatial and other principles learned in all tasks, are listed in the first column for each level, while suggested *materials* are listed in the second column. Many of the materials are readily available in the ordinary day care center and school (or home if parents are involved) and can be secured with little difficulty. Some of the materials may require some preparation, however, including fashioning the necessary tools. Suggestions for materials to utilize for fashioning tools are sometimes indicated (e.g., tinker toy sets to make retrieval tools) and the more interested and inventive supervisors, caregivers, and teachers will always find materials for making devices of their own.

The following are a few simple rules to observe in setting up tasks to foster both learning and enjoyment:

1. *Setting.* In order to avoid distraction, find some quiet corner of the playroom, or a separate small room with the necessary materials prepared in advance.

2. *Approach.* The approach to problem solving activities is often more flexible than usual for teaching concept learning sequences in the knowledge curriculum. The high appeal problem solving in simple tasks holds for children, moreover, frequently reduces the amount of dramatic play needed, though the scattered motivation of some children is more easily engaged through defining tasks in terms of play in social roles and imaginary situations.

It is particularly important to minimize the amount of adult intrusion into the child's efforts to figure out and experiment with a problem. The teacher's job is primarily to present the problem for the child to work on. If a problem is well selected for the child's level and materials are set out so that an interesting, visible goal (e.g., an appealing toy) is *only* obtainable through organizing certain means at hand, motivation will be high and little guidance will be necessary. More guidance will naturally be needed with overdependent, passive and hyperactive children, in group situations, and at some phases more than others. Aside from tending to behavioral problems, guidance is useful for encouraging the child and for providing significant cues.

Although materials are laid out to make critical features and relations to ends evident, depending on age and skill, many problems require some statement of the nature of the task, what the child is to do. Brief instructions, perhaps accompanied by a sample demonstration or indication of an important part of a tool will arouse the most interest. As the child plays with a problem, further suggestions are useful, such as when a child continues to pursue a useless path, makes no headway, becomes too frustrated, or the materials somehow become so cluttered they obscure important possibilities. Drawing attention to selected critical parts and relations (analyzing and synthesizing) of a problem through pointing and demonstrating, and or asking pointed questions, helps young children to develop more than making suggestions or doing the whole task for the child without breaking it down. Remember, the aim is to stimulate the child to become an independent problem solver through learning general principles, not simply to solve the problem at hand. It is not amiss to ask the child to state a general rule occasionally, usually as soon as she/he solves a problem, perhaps asking her/him to do it again for fun. But such demands should be sparing even with highly verbal and conceptual preschool age children, and often aided by the adult stating (but not overstressing) the principle in simple terms.

GROUP WORK

Problem solving activities particularly lend themselves to teaching children the value of cooperation. The solution to many problems, such as reaching an object on a high shelf through piling blocks, is more easily realized with more than one child. Assembling or making tools, carrying a large or awkward object, and even searching for necessary tools (e.g., puzzle pieces, retrieval tools) are both easier and more fun when two or three children work together. The problem is, of course, to temper the intensity of competition and conflict through such methods as taking turns and designing collaborative tasks. The ideal circumstances are those in which a problem can be solved *only* by two (or more) children working together (e.g., pulling up a full bucket with a rope that is too heavy for one child, spreading out a sizable rug, or operating a toy or bell that requires two levers or buttons to work). Illustrations of such tasks are included in the series.

Group work also provides children the opportunity for repeated experience with the same or similar problems. When children are asked to take turns, they usually gain added experience through observing one another. This process stimulates the formation of mental hypotheses, with which they can experiment when their turn arrives. But children can also be assigned the role of teacher, arranging materials and setting the problem for other children. Such experience further enriches their knowledge of task *principles* and enhances their motivation considerably. Since setting a problem is much more difficult than solving one, even when the child is familiar with the problem, added teacher aid is usually needed. Be sure every child gets some leadership experience, however limited his social and problem solving skills.

CULTURAL AND SEX DIFFERENCES

Children from different cultures, social classes, and boys and girls all bring to every problem different degrees of familiarity with mechanical, household, and other types of tasks, or even motivation for solving arranged problems at all. It is important that every child be insured a broad range of experience on all types and areas of problems. The question is particularly acute for boys and girls, to break through the culturally traditional stereotypes of "boy" and "girl" type activities. Problem solving in spatial activities is too often confined to boys and persistent effort is needed to encourage the participation of girls, who may also be subjected to exclusionary pressures by boys or traditionalist (in effect sexist) attitudes of the adults.

Problem Solving
Sequences

I. TRANSPORTING OBJECTS

A. RETRIEVING OBJECTS

Special Concepts (Rules)	Materials	Learning Tasks	Concept Generalization Tasks
		Basic Problem	
Objects can be re-retrieved with tools in different ways.	1. Retrieval and carrying tools. 2. Appealing goal objects.	Retrieving desired objects.	Use similar tools and goals objects under different conditions.
		Level I. 0–6+ Months	
1. Perceiving *features* of objects. 2. *Object permanence* (aspects).	1. Sensory motor systems. 2. Small goal objects (toys) and appealing objects varying in color, brightness, movement, sound-making properties, texture, weight, size, smell, etc.	Present object alternately for infant to see and follow, handle, hear, mouth, and smell.	1. Vary angle, speed, direction, and type of goal objects. 2. Vary setting and infant's position.
		Level II. 2–9 Months	
1. *Interrelating features* of objects. 2. *Object permanence* (aspects).	Same as 1 and 2 above.	Same as above but help infant use his senses in combination, i.e., see what she/he touches and vice versa; see what he/she hears, etc.	1. Same as 1 and 2 above. 2. Also vary all combinations of senses used.
		Level III. 4–15 Months	
Objects (seen/heard) can be retrieved by the hands as tools.	1. Hand-eye system. 2. Hand-ear-eye system. 3. Small goal objects as in 1 and 2 above.	Present each goal object within reach for infants to retrieve by hand (as a tool): a. Objects she/he sees.	1. Vary angle, distance and height (within and just beyond reach), type of goal objects and infant's position. 2. Vary sound and

I. TRANSPORTING OBJECTS (cont.)

Special Concepts (Rules)	Materials	Learning Tasks	Concept Generalization Tasks
		Level III. 4–15 Months (cont.)	
		b. Objects she/he hears.	visibility of noise making objects (e.g., sound object to side and back of infant).
		Level IV. 9–30+ Months	
1. Objects beyond reach can be *retrieved with tools of* different kinds.	1. Small goal objects as in Level I. 2. Retrieval type tools: a. Toy hoes and rakes. b. Sticks—straight and bent (e.g., twigs). c. Tinker toy sticks (one or two lengths with a knob and/or elbow on the end). d. String with a loop (lasso). e. Sticks or rods with hooks or loops to hook an object. f. Spoons, shovels, scoops, flat boards, or cardboard. g. Forks and spears (under close supervision). 3. Barriers as needed (e.g., fences, tables, high shelves).	1. Place each goal object beyond reach so as to require retrieval devices (tools). For example, place child behind a barrier, or goal object on a high shelf or across a table. 2. Place retrieval tool(s) at hand.	1. Same as 1 above. 2. Vary placement of tools. 3. Vary type of tools.
		Level V. 15–36+ Months	
1. *Alternatives:* a. Different means (tools) to the same end are often available.	1. Small goal objects as before. 2. Retrieval tools as in 2 above. 3. Larger goal objects,	1. Same as 1 above but with a choice of two tools. 2. Place each carrying device near child,	1. Same as 1 above. 2. Vary number (two to five) of tool choices; and/or include tools with obvi-

continued

I. TRANSPORTING OBJECTS (cont.)

Special Concepts (Rules)	Materials	Learning Tasks	Concept Generalization Tasks

Level V.   15–36+ Months (cont.)

Special Concepts (Rules)	Materials	Learning Tasks	Concept Generalization Tasks
b. Some work better than others. 2. Objects beyond reach can be retrieved by *transporting* (carrying). 3. *Different means* (carriers) can be used to transport things. 4. *Hidden objects* can be found. 5. *Picture representation* rules.	some too large, heavy, or awkward to carry alone. 4. Carrying devices: a. Boxes, pans, buckets, and other containers to carry numerous small objects. b. Miniature vehicles (cars, trucks, trains, etc.) to carry objects by rolling (wheels save effort). c. Child size vehicles, e.g., wagons, carts, trucks. d. Suitcases and trunks (for trips). e. Nets, cloth, bags, and paper (to wrap). f. Trays, boards, lids, etc. g. Ropes, loops, wire string, etc., to loop or fasten. h. Balls to roll. i. Pulley system.	and large goal objects at a distance. 3. Alternately, have child move each (large) goal object by sliding (e.g., blocks, chairs), rolling (e.g., balls, cylinders); moving end over end (e.g., large boxes, blocks); or hoisting (e.g., bucket with rope-pulley). 4. Present objects hidden from sight in containers or behind various screens and other large obscuring objects.	ous differences in effectiveness (e.g., hoe versus rake for retrieving sand, stick with hook versus straight stick to retrieve a ring). 3. Vary placement of carrying devices. 4. Vary methods of moving and type of carrying devices according to size, weight, shape, and number of goal objects. 5. Include occasional noncarrying objects and two or more carrying objects to complicate choices. 6. Vary angle, and position of hidden goal objects (to be retrieved without and with carrying devices) as follows: a. Vary position, distance, and type of containers for goal objects. b. Displace goal objects to cupboards, nearby rooms, etc. c. Set up tasks with two or more goal objects to retrieve, especially, in *practical tasks* of getting

I. TRANSPORTING OBJECTS (cont.)

Special Concepts *(Rules)*	*Materials*	*Learning Tasks*	*Concept* *Generalization* *Tasks*
	Level V. 15–36+ Months (cont.)		
			needed toys, art material, etc., from storage.
			7. Show *pictures* of tools and carrying devices, asking child to select the/a tool (by pointing) that will work. Offer choices between two and gradually three to five pictured choices, including nontool (or noncarrier) materials. After choosing, ask the child to perform the task with a tool (carrier) like the one he/she chose in the picture, letting him/her correct his/her own errors if possible. Pictures of tools can be made by cutting out magazine (mail order catalog, etc.) pictures and pasting sets on colored paper or cardboard.
	Level VI. 24–48+ Months		
1. *Tool making*: Tools can be made in order to retrieve things beyond reach. 2. *Tools*, which singly won't work, can be *used together* to attain goals (i.e., dual con-	1. Small and large goal objects as in 1 and 2 above. 2. Sets of tool (and carrier) *components* to be placed in appropriate combinations for the child to as-	1. Same general task conditions as before (i.e., goal objects beyond reach and tools or carriers near child). 2. But present *components* of tools and	1. Same types of variations in goal objects and placements as before. 2. Vary combinations of retrieval tool and carrier components to broaden and increase

continued

I. TRANSPORTING OBJECTS (cont.)

Special Concepts (Rules)	Materials	Learning Tasks	Concept Generalization Tasks

Level VI.   24–48+ Months (cont.)

trol, contingency operation). 3. Different *combinations* of means can achieve the same purpose (i.e., retrieve a goal object). 4. *Pictorial* and *Language representation* rules.	semble or with which to fashion a tool, e.g.: a. Two (or more) sticks (needed to reach as far as the goal objects), which can be screwed or fastened together (e.g., tinker toys, snap or hook connection stick toys). b. Two (or more) sticks to make a rake. c. Making a loop, crook, or ring with a soft wire to lasso or hook an object. d. Boxes, blocks, etc., for piling to reach a high object. e. Two (or more) lengths of rope, wire, string, etc., for tying together to reach distant goal object (e.g., pulling up a pail or basket). f. Stick, rope and hook. g. Carpentry tools, boards, nails, etc., for fashioning needed retrieval tools.	carriers, which require *joint use* or assembling to retrieve a goal object.	complexity of problem solving demands (e.g., increasing number of parts and steps to goal). 3. Show *pictures* (or drawings) of people faced with retrieval problems. Discuss with child(ren) how they would go about retrieving the objects (what means, including inventing tools, and principles involved).

I. TRANSPORTING OBJECTS (cont.)

B. PLACING-TARGETING OBJECTS

Special Concepts (Rules)	Materials	Learning Tasks	Concept Generalization Tasks
		Basic Problem	
Objects can be *placed* or *targeted* in different ways (positioning control, gravity, trajection).	1. Placing, transporting, and targeting. 2. Goal objects.	1. Placing-positioning objects.	Use similar tools and goal objects under varying conditions.

Level I–II.   0–9+ Months

Level I and II object concepts and exploratory-manipulatory activities identical to those of Retrieval Series.

Level III.   9–18+ Months

Special Concepts (Rules)	Materials	Learning Tasks	Concept Generalization Tasks
1. Object can be placed-targeted with the hands (undifferentiated).	1. Hand-eye system. 2. Hand-eye-ear system. 3. Small goal objects that vary in color, brightness, movement, sound making, texture, weight, etc. 4. Placing and targeting objects, e.g., boxes, jars, and other containers; cutout shapes of colored construction paper, cloth, wood, etc.; any defined area (e.g., painted spot, table top, area rug, chair seat, etc.).	1. Present each object within reach for infant to place in/on a designated, nearby object, container, surface area, etc. 2. Select occasional placing objects and areas or containers that make distinctive sounds when object is placed or dropped (e.g., wooden balls in jar, bell, etc.).	1. Vary angle, distance and height (within and just beyond reach) and type and size of both placement areas and placing objects. 2. Vary placement position (e.g., on, in, under, beside, behind, near, etc.). 3. Select different combinations of sound-making materials.

Level III.   9–18+ Months

Special Concepts (Rules)	Materials	Learning Tasks	Concept Generalization Tasks
1. *Targeting* objects. 2. *Placing* with *tools*.	1. Same as 1–4 above. 2. Placing tools, e.g.: a. Spoons, shovels and other elongated devices for placing objects in areas be-	1. Present small objects as in 1 and 2 above, *alternately* to place (releasing object in contact with area) or target (dropping object from a slight height).	1. Vary angle, distance and height, etc., as in 1 and 2 above. 2. Vary barriers and accessibility to placing and target areas. In the case of targeting activities shift from

continued

I. TRANSPORTING OBJECTS (cont.)

Special Concepts (Rules)	Materials	Learning Tasks	Concept Generalization Tasks
	Level IV. 12–30+ *Months* (cont.)		
	yond reach (e.g., on a high shelf, from behind or across a table). b. Hoes, rakes, boards, sticks, etc., for pushing.	2. Place small objects and tools near child for him/her to place objects in/on designated areas at a distance.	dropping to rolling, sliding, etc., onto an area or into a container (on its side) or tossing (e.g., into a nearby box).
	3. Barriers as needed (e.g., fences, tables, high shelves, etc.).		
	Level V. 18–36+ *Months*		
1. Objects can be *placed* beyond reach by carrying (transporting). 2. *Alternatives: different means* for carrying (transporting) can be employed. 3. Objects can be *hidden*, stored, put away, etc. 4. *Ordering and classifying.* 5. *Pictorial representation* rules.	Essentially the same as carrying devices and vehicles used in *retrieving* heavy, numerous, or awkward objects.	1. Essentially the same as for retrieving at Level V, except that the task is to carry or transport objects *to* a designated spot away from child (e.g., task is to lower an object with a net, rope, or bucket instead of hoisting one). 2. Have child hide objects in containers or behind objects as before.	1. Much the same type of variations as for object retrieval at Level V. 2. Vary distance, type of hiding place (e.g., containers, cupboards, nearby room, under rugs, etc.), and number of object-placement matches. 3. *Practical problem variations* are putting things away (i.e., for clean up, tidying, storage), such as at the end of free play period after snack or meal, etc. Vary number and order of objects to put away, including the number of different positions in which objects must be stored (e.g., different utensils, dishes, colored paints, types of blocks, and other toys).

I. TRANSPORTING OBJECTS (cont.)

Special Concepts (Rules)	*Materials*	*Learning Tasks*	*Concept Generalization Tasks*

Level V.   18–36+ Months (cont.)

			4. Use *pictures* as in object retrieval problem series (Level V).

Level VI.   24–48+ Months

Special Concepts (Rules)	*Materials*	*Learning Tasks*	*Concept Generalization Tasks*
1. Same focus on *tool making* and *joint use* of objects as tools as in Level VI in Object Retrieval Tasks. 2. *Complex targeting* —aiming through *distal space.*[a] 3. *Pictorial* and *language representation* rules.	1. Various types of targets, e.g., paper bull's eyes, circles drawn on ground or floor, toy animals, empty cardboard boxes, containers, or ordinary small objects set up in an appropriate setting. 2. Various projectiles or instruments for targeting, e.g., pins and donkey tails, rubber suction darts, crayons to aim at paper, water squirters (syringes), balls, bean bags, etc., soft balls, bean bags, or balloons suspended on a string to swing at other suspended objects or knock a soft object off a shelf, etc.	1. Provide a large space (corner of room or outdoors) free of activity and danger to children for setting up targets and projecting (tossing, throwing, etc.), objects from two plus feet away. 2. Have children take turns aiming and targeting; supervise closely all tossing-throwing activities.	1. Vary type of projectile, target and distance up to ten or more feet (three or more meters) for three to five year olds. 2. Make up pictures (or drawings) of people in placing-targeting scenes and discuss the alternatives, combinations, and principles involved, as in object retrieval problems (Level VI).

continued

[a] Unfortunately, distal targeting is associated with weapons play and concepts of violence which are heavily reinforced by the commercial mass media. The spatial control skills involved are nonetheless useful and the antisocial concepts and play can be minimized by the projectile instruments chosen (e.g., water syringes versus water pistol), careful control over the activities, and maintaining a strong distinction between "object targeting" and "people "targeting."

II. BARRIER—DETOUR PROBLEMS [a]

Special Concepts (Rules)	Materials	Learning Tasks	Concept Generalization Tasks
		Basic Problem	
There are often physical barriers and obstacles to goals that can be overcome in different ways.	1. Appealing goal objects. 2. Physical barriers and obstacles of all kinds.	Removing or bypassing obstacles to goals.	Use a variety of obstacles under varying conditions.
		Level I. 6–15+ Months	
(Apparent) impediments can be bypassed by *reaching beyond* (over) them.	1. Sensory motor system (eye-hand-ear). 2. Miscellaneous small objects and toys of all kinds to place in the route of reaching for a goal object. 3. Small appealing goal objects of all kinds.	1. Placing an appealing goal object in front of infant. 2. Simultaneously place a single object —*preferably less interesting to the child* between the goal and the child.	1. Vary the type of both the goal objects and the intervening objects in size, color, shape, etc. 2. Vary the spacing between objects and distance from child (to a few feet or quarter meters) 3. As skill develops, increase the size (and number) of the intervening objects in comparison to the goal objects, but not to a point of presenting difficulty reaching over them.
		Level II. 8–24+ Months	
Barriers or obstacles can be overcome by *removing* them.	1. Same as 1 and 3 above. 2. Physical barriers, small and light enough for child to move, but large enough to prevent direct access to goal, e.g., moderate sized blocks and boxes; balls and vehicles; large toys	1. Place a removable barrier in between child and an appealing goal object, simultaneously, in such a way that there is no space to go around the barrier.	1. Vary both the type of goal object and barrier by size, color, shape, angle and distance (from child and between goal and barrier). 2. Set alternative problems, e.g., retrieving an object covered with other objects or

[a] While physical barriers and other obstacles are present in many sorts of tasks, especially in object retrieval problems, special focus on overcoming obstacles (as against focus on tools) enhances awareness and fosters general competence and cognitive adaptiveness in what is often the core of a problem.

II. BARRIER—DETOUR PROBLEMS (cont.)

Special Concepts (Rules)	Materials	Learning Tasks	Concept Generalization Tasks

Level II. 8–24+ Months (cont.)

| | (e.g., wheel or push toys); small furniture; boards; pillows; pile of dirt, sand, etc. 3. Other obstacles, e.g., sand, dirt, water in a jar; miscellaneous toys and objects to pile on goal object (on the floor, in a hole or in a box, etc.). | | material (on the floor, in a hole in the ground or sand or in a container of water or sand to be emptied), limiting obstacles to two to three or a thin covering of dirt, etc. |

Level III.   10–30+ Months

| 1. Barriers or obstacles can be overcome through taking *detours*. 2. Barriers or obstacles (when difficult or impassable) can be overcome by making them irrelevant, i.e., finding *substitute goal objects* to serve the same purpose or function (i.e., means to a further end). | 1. Same as 1 above. 2. Physical barriers, too heavy, big, or unwieldy for child to move, e.g., large boxes, blocks, furniture, climbing apparatus, partitions, toy shelves, painting easels, etc. | 1. Same as in Level II above, but the barrier should be immovable (by child) and there should be room to detour. 2. Same as 1 but with detours difficult or impossible. Place a less obvious substitute goal object at hand. | 1. Vary goal objects, barriers and conditions as before. 2. Present some barriers without room to bypass, but which can be climbed over (e.g., furniture, pile of boxes, climbing apparatus) or crawled through (e.g., tunnel, hole in fence, etc.). 3. When used, vary the substitute goal objects in visibility, accessibility (minor barriers) and obviousness of function (e.g., a curved stick for a rake, colored string for a ribbon). |

Level IV.   15–36+ Months

| *Complex barriers* can be overcome through removing by *dismantling* them. | 1. Same as 1 above. 2. Complex barrier structures that can be dismantled, but are too heavy, large, or made of too many | Place barriers and goal objects as in Level II problems, that is, without any space for child to detour. | 1. Vary goal objects, barriers and conditions as before. 2. As skill develops, present barriers which are fastened tightly |

continued

II. BARRIER—DETOUR PROBLEMS (cont.)

Special Concepts (Rules)	Materials	Learning Tasks	Concept Generalization Tasks

Level IV.   15–36+ Months (cont.)

| | parts to move as a whole, e.g., large block structures (hollow or unit blocks) or other modular structure (e.g., leggos, tinker toy); piles or walls of furniture; wall of large cardboard cartons; wooden fences with removable boards; appropriate tools, (e.g., hammer, pry). | | together and do not come apart too easily (e.g., fitted in, dove tailed, pegged, tightly interlocking parts; cartons or thin boards that can be sawn, etc.). |

Level V.   18–48+ Months

| 1. Complex barriers can be overcome by *special mechanisms* means (e.g., unfastening and/or opening doors; water taps, etc.).
 2. Barriers may *require coordinated operations* to overcome (i.e., two hand sequential interaction-dual control, contingency functioning).
 3. *Pictorial coding rules.* | 1. Same as 1 above.
 2. A variety of barriers (e.g., boxes, jars, and other containers; walls), with different types of access (e.g., lids, tops, doors, windows, match boxes, bureau drawers, etc.) and/or mechanisms to be unfastened (e.g., simple removable or hinge lids; screw and snap tops; drawers; sliding doors and windows; latches, locks, hooks and eyes; bolt, button, and lever type doors including jack-in-the-boxes, vending, gumball type dispensers, etc.). | 1. Place appealing goal object inside container while child watches, then fasten opening and present for him to play with and retrieve goal object.
 2. Special guidance may be useful when fastening mechanism requires (two hand) sequenced coordination (e.g., opening drawers, hinge tops, screw tops, slide bolts, sliding doors on the slant, key-doorknob, etc.). | 1. Vary type of goal objects, form of access, and type of fastening mechanisms, settings, etc.; use some transparent containers (e.g., jars) and walls (e.g., windows, hard plastic).
 2. Use fence or wall type barriers with various types of windows and doors and different fastening mechanisms. Eliminate detour or dismantling alternatives.
 3. As skill develops, hide a goal object without child watching, merely telling him/her that one is in or behind barrier.
 4. To give additional practice in fastening- |

II. BARRIER—DETOUR PROBLEMS (cont.)

Special Concepts (Rules)	*Materials*	*Learning Tasks*	*Concept Generalization Tasks*

Level V.   18–48+ Months (cont.)

unfastening (other than child's spontaneous interest through play), have children take turns setting up problems for other children.
5. Show *pictures* of (one to three) barriers or obstacles (in relation to goal objects) for child to choose (by pointing) which one will successfully block a path to a goal object. Include choices with two more or equally effective barriers and obstacles. Then have child try to overcome a barrier of the type he/she chose, to test its utility as a barrier.

Level VI.   24–48+ Months

Special Concepts (Rules)	*Materials*	*Learning Tasks*	*Concept Generalization Tasks*
1. Barriers may require *coordinated, sequential actions* or detours to overcome (i.e., contingency, two or more step problems). 2. *Pictorial* and *language* representation rules.	1. Same as 1 above. 2. Same as 2 above, but all with two or more steps required to gain access to container or through barrier wall (e.g., box lids, doors, etc., with two or more latches, locks, and other fasteners, buttons, or levers to push, etc.; regression series of containers, i.e., boxes within boxes, nesting	1. Essentially the same as 1 and 2 above, but more demonstrations may be needed.	1. Same range of variations as above, plus increasing the number of steps as skill develops (e.g., number of latches of different types, doors, lids, containers within containers, etc.). 2. *Mazes.* Start with one or two turn mazes, increasing length and intricacy of route to goal object gradually. Only older

continued

II. BARRIER—DETOUR PROBLEMS (cont.)

Special Concepts (Rules)	Materials	Learning Tasks	Concept Generalization Tasks
	Level VI. 24–48+ Months (cont.)		
	eggs and dolls; multi-block Japanese puzzles; tracing or tunnel mazes, including those made with unit blocks and arrangements of movable toy shelves and other furniture for child to walk or crawl through).		or more skilled children can be introduced to crayon/pencil/stylus tracing mazes, requiring adherence to arbitrary social rules (i.e., for child simply not to reach directly for goal object). 3. Make up pictures (or drawings) of barrier or obstacle scenes for children to discuss alternatives of how to remove or bypass, and principles involved, as in object retrieval problems (Level VI).

III. TOOL USING

Special Concepts (Rules)	Materials	Learning Tasks	Concept Generalization Tasks
	Basic Problem		
1. Environmental control and regulation. 2. Extending human power. 3. Causality-alternative means and ends.	1. Hand-eye system. 2. Tools of all kinds.	Operating tools of all kinds to produce specific effects.	Varying conditions, tools for the same end, and ends with the same tool.
	Level I. 0–12+ Months		
1. *Things move.* 2. *Things can be moved* by various types of actions.	1. Free swinging mobiles: commercial and handmade (e.g., paper, cloth, and cardboard cutouts; miniature figures;	1. Colorful mobiles close to infant's visual field. 2. Suspend mobiles with a long cord and handle that, when	1. Vary mobiles, settings, angle, and distance from infant. 2. Vary type of activating mechanism, and part of body by

III. TOOL USING (cont.)

Special Concepts (Rules)	Materials	Learning Tasks	Concept Generalization Tasks

Level I.   0–12+ Months (cont.)

	match stick designs; two and three dimensional, etc.). 2. Same—but with devices for infant to activate, e.g., long cord and knob to infants' hand; lever or button near hand; air bulb under pillow which activates a mobile through an attached rubber tube; crib movement, etc.	manipulated, activates mobiles.	which infant activates, e.g., foot, hand, head, and body activation; etc.

Level II.   6–24+ Months

| 1. Things can be *moved unidirectionally* and *reversed* (back and forth, up and down, sideways, etc.). 2. Things and movements can be *started and stopped*. 3. Things can be *grasped* and *released*. | 1. Miscellaneous small objects of varying shape, color, size, etc. 2. Wheel toys, balls, and cylinders. 3. Commercial and home made toys and gadgets that move in different ways, e.g., toys suspended by string; levers that pull back and forth, up and down, etc.; drawers, push-pull buttons, etc. 4. Crayons or similar markers. | 1. Interest infant in imitating various types of unidirectional and reversible movements, i.e.,

a. Pushing, pulling, then pushing and pulling the same object back and forth or sideways.
b. Raising, lowering, then alternately raising and lowering the same object. | 1. Vary the type of objects, setting, angle, speed, length, and specific means of moving, e.g., sliding, rolling and swinging objects; operating gadgets; inserting and removing objects in and from container holes; crayon marking; picking up, dropping from various heights, etc. 2. Pause and restart, and pause, release, regrasp, and restart at various points in a cycle. 3. Vary hand employed and sometimes use two hands. |

Level III.   12–36+ Months

| 1. *Tools* are designed to perform *particular functions*. There are *different tools* to per- | Various types of simple (1 step) tools, e.g.: | Set up tasks requiring single, specific tools, placing the correct tool at hand. | 1. Vary tasks, tools and settings over a broad range. 2. As skill and under- |

continued

III. TOOL USING (cont.)

			Concept Generalization
Special Concepts (Rules)	*Materials*	*Learning Tasks*	*Tasks*

Level III.   12–36+ Months (cont.)

form different functions. 2. *Similar devices* can perform the *same functions*.	a. Garden tools (e.g., rakes, hoes, trowels). b. Kitchen utensils (e.g., spoons, forks, spatula, pots, pans). c. Eating utensils (e.g., spoons, forks, dishes, napkins). d. Carpentry tools (e.g., hammer, screw driver with nail or screw already started, as in toy work benches). e. Plumbing tools (e.g., wrenches, as in toy work benches).		standing are demonstrated, place choices between pairs of tools (and later) three or more tools for the same task. 3. Set up tasks with the appropriate tool missing, but with at least one plausible alternative provided, e.g., a dull knife for a screwdriver, a screwdriver for puttying, a stone for hammering, etc.

Level IV.   15–36+ Months

1. Things, especially round things, can be *turned, in two directions* (balls in any direction). 2. *Wheels* on rods turn in *stable rotations*. 3. *Screws* (bolts are fastened by turning in a single direction (and vice versa).	1. Circular turning levers (handles on wheels), steering wheels (large and small), wheels on vehicles, any object that turns on an axle, suspended objects, etc. 2. Wooden screw bolt toys; cylinders and balls, some that protrude from insets and can be turned—place marks on edge or side to show progression; hardware gadgets with screw bolts. 3. Crayons, finger paint, paint brushes. 4. Miscellaneous small objects.	1. Offer for play and/or interest infant in imitating turning levers and miscellaneous objects, one at a time. 2. Demonstrate how to turn and release (alternating steps) in hand turning of wooden screw bolts.	1. Vary type of turning levers, wheels, cylinders, objects, crayons for scribble, circles and circle objects suspended on string, etc., speed direction, angle, etc. 2. Vary the hand employed, occasionally use two hands. 3. Draw attention to how interlocking gears work by removing and replacing connecting gear wheels. 4. Start and stop turns at any point in a cycle. 5. Spin wheels when possible.

III. TOOL USING (cont.)

Special Concepts (Rules)	Materials	Learning Tasks	Concept Generalization Tasks

Level IV.   15–36+ Months (cont.)

	5. Multiple interlocking gear toys.		6. Offer large metal screw bolts with hardware gadgets, and similar screw devices.

Level V.   18–48+ Months

Special Concepts (Rules)	Materials	Learning Tasks	Concept Generalization Tasks
1. Complex tools require two to three *steps* and/or *coordinated* (two handed) *manipulations*. 2. Again, concept or similar devices performing same function. 3. *Pictorial representation* rules.	Various types of complex tools, e.g.: a. Garden tools (e.g., full size shovels, spades, toy or large shovels and buckets; clippers). b. Kitchen and household (e.g., broom and dustpan; mop and waterbucket; eggbeater, scissors). c. Eating utensils (e.g., knife and fork, cup and saucer). d. Carpentry tools (e.g., pliers, hammer-nails, screwdriver-screws, saw, brace and bit, vise, wood clamps-glue, wood plane). e. Plumbing tools (e.g., adjustable wrenches, pipe lengths and joints, tin shears, "plumber's helper").	Same as above, using complex tools. More demonstrations and guidance may be necessary initially in actual task performance.	1. Same as 1 and 2, Level III, using appropriate complex tools. 2. Same as 3, Level III, with complex tool alternatives (e.g., vise for wood clamps; rag for broom, and cardboard for dustpan, fork for eggbeater; clamps for wrenches). 3. Provide pictures of various tools to choose among, then select from a real set, as in object retrieval problems (Level V).

Level VI.   24–48+ Months

Special Concepts (Rules)	Materials	Learning Tasks	Concept Generalization Tasks
1. Same as above, but using *multistep sequences* and *interdependent* operations. 2. Complex *struc-*	Various sets of tools and appropriate materials, e.g.: a. Garden tools (e.g., shovels, hoes, weeding	1. Set out tools and materials needed, together with discussion of construction project.	1. Vary type of projects. 2. Develop more elaborate projects extending over several

continued

III. TOOL USING (cont.)

Special Concepts (Rules)	Materials	Learning Tasks	Concept Generalization Tasks

Level VI.   24–48+ Months (cont.)

tures can be constructed by placing and executing with tools in a series of coordinated steps.
3. *Pictorial* and *language representation* rules.

forks, garden area, seeds, water, fertilizers).
b. Kitchen and household (e.g., pots, pans, utensils, ingredients necessary to make bread, cookies, or other food).
c. Eating utensils (sets of dishes, utensils, napkins, place mats, etc., for actual or play meals and snacks).
d. Carpentry tools (e.g., hammer, saw, nails, screwdriver, screws, ruler, square or tape measure, wood, etc., for building crude boxes, boats, tables, chairs, etc.).
e. Plumbing tools (e.g., wrenches, pipe lengths and joints, pipe seal to assemble simple pipe system to pour water through— from one bucket to another at a distance).

2. Offer project goal choices; discuss.
3. Considerable guidance and demonstration likely to be needed along the way but encourage children's decision making and experimentation on tool selection and component step operation.
4. Many projects are easier to stimulate and complete through two to three children working together.
5. Initially select tasks that can be completed in one or two sessions.

days, as skills and interest develop.
3. Set up component tasks for two (or more) children to work on together, (e.g., two children alternately holding and pulling tape measures, holding square and marking line, holding board and sawing, holding bowl and stirring, holding dustpan and broom).
4. Make up pictures (or drawings) of people faced with tool-using construction problems and discuss choices, procedures, steps, and principles, as in object retrieval problems (Level VI).

3

Language
Curriculum

GENERAL CHARACTERISTICS

From earliest times, children everywhere have learned to talk through the spontaneous communication of adults in daily life. By age four most of them acquire a working foundation of their language. They can make their wants known and talk with others about familiar things around them.

Yet the informal curriculum traditional to all cultures has always produced problems and day care may further undermine the effectiveness of the traditional home program. Under the informal approach, many children in every community develop speech problems of one sort or another, which a little preventive planning might frequently minimize. Few children, moreover, develop their full potential for language mastery. But day care itself adds new hazards to language development, which are apt to be of a special kind that may go unnoticed. The problem centers on the potential reduction of adult language attention individually available to each child.

Even in large families, infants frequently experience the undivided attention of the mother and extensive exposure to older siblings already fairly skilled in language. In contrast, in all except the rarest of day care centers, the infant must routinely share attention with several other infants facing the same age needs for language stimulation, and who thus also provide poor models for learning to talk. The problem for development is of course similar for other types of learning. But the risk is probably greatest in the area of language, because the environment does not naturally provide the same incentive to use language that it does for learning other concepts through play. As a result, the arrival of sociodramatic play may be delayed and the quality of language employed by the play group may be lowered, further retarding language development.

One evident solution to this problem is to add the company of older children, as in a family type grouping. But the cumulative effects of less adult attention also indicates the need for a specially planned language program. The methods should certainly keep as much of the informality of the home as possible while insuring frequency and regularity.

Like problem solving, language stimulation is built into the routines of basic caregiving, and is indispensable for guided learning activities. This chapter will discuss in detail the activities in day care suitable for stimulating language learning and outline techniques and curriculum sequences for fostering language development. The general approach to language learning is organized in terms of common rules of language sound, words, and sentence structure, as much as possible related to meaning.

LANGUAGE LEARNING ACTIVITIES

It will be useful first to list the types of activities in day care for which to plan language learning and review methods briefly before outlining the curriculum. Aside from guided learning and the basic care routines, there are at least five types of situations for providing language experiences. These are (1) adult-child social play, (2) object exploratory and manipulatory inter-action, (3) picture-story and poetry sessions, including oral language ac-tivities, (4) labeling trips around the day care center, and (5) labeling excur-sions outside the center, in the neighborhood and elsewhere. As their name implies, the last two types are intended to broaden the child's grasp of lan-guage in different contexts. While the first three include some broadening, they are also designed to serve special purposes. The first is to develop lan-guage in the all-important sphere of social relations. The second is to pro-vide a quiet, concentrated context, helpful for bringing into focus the various rules of language structure, but especially how language represents things. The third type introduces the infant to the world of picture representation, learning the rules for picturing things on flat surfaces, but equally important, is leading the child toward the world of ideas and aesthetics through books.

Poetry, particularly simple rhymes, is valuable for developing awareness of sound patterns, and thus precision and aesthetic rhythms in language. Poetry and prose enrich the child's ability for accurate description, under-standing time and event sequences (a story line), and in general develop the imaginative and abstractive powers through the use of imagery and metaphor. Like the object play activities, picture-story activities also hold many pos-sibilities for drawing attention to the particularities of language rules (for example, rules for describing features of things with adjectives, such as long or tall; or relations between terms in sentences making up a basic action-event structure, such as "a child holding a guinea pig" (subject-action-object relations). In the end, picture books also serve as one of the most powerful broadening sources, because the variety of difficult-to-visit materials and situations, from factories to tropical islands, that become accessible is prac-tically endless. Moreover, pictures and particularly drawings can select and display things in ways that make them clearer and easier to understand in real life.

Oral language activities, telling stories and reciting poems, are valuable for developing memory and the creative, imaginative aspects of language in aesthetic media. They are particularly strong in developing personalized styles of expression and may lead later to creative writing and writing poetry.

REVIEW OF LANGUAGE INTERACTION METHODS

Each activity presents some variation in approach, but in all activities the style is much the same, language is used freely but selectively in a series of *easy interactions between caregiver and child.* The aim is to use the infant's responses to the teacher's initiatives, as well as the infant's spontaneous inter-est in the materials and events of prepared situations as a basis for language stimulation. Responding to the infant's responses and spontaneous actions by appropriate actions and language is as important as maintaining a general line of productive teaching activity. When a balance is maintained between the caregiver's efforts to label and manipulate materials and the child's manipulative play and responses, an ideal flow of learning and interest for the child is maintained. Five- to twenty-minute activity sessions for indoor sessions are the usual range, depending on the child's age, usual attention span, and various other circumstances.

Language sessions deal with particulars following the pattern of ordinary guided concept learning sessions, but the focus is on language concepts rather than on concepts about the environment. Language concepts take two forms, the rules by which environmental and other idea concepts are labeled (e.g., a given word represents a variety of similar objects, such as "bottle") and the internal rules of language structure itself. (The latter rules, the rules of sound patterns, words, and sentence organization, will be presented in simplified form in the curriculum outline.) Various aspects of language concepts are useful to emphasize at different stages of the child's language learning. But infant language teaching is mainly a process of combining attention to word and phrase labels with their relation to examples the objects and actions they refer to. Thus, while more attention is paid to what and how things are said than in ordinary concept learning, the caregiver's words are generally closely timed to the actions she/he, the child, or some other person is performing. At the beginning, language is learned most easily through using it as a tool for action.

Language learning needs a social atmosphere of casualness, fun, and sensitivity to individual differences. Quiet corners or rooms with prepared materials are useful for the object manipulation, story, and social play sessions, but the labeling trips naturally move through many settings in and outside the center.

Like so much other learning, language play activities can many times be carried out in *small groups*. Language activities lend themselves to a caregiver interacting with several children in labeling, word, and sentence play, once the infant has grasped the idea of a word standing for (symbolizing) an object or idea. At this stage, children become increasingly enthusiastic in cooperating and/or taking turns to locate objects a caregiver names, to perform an action a caregiver uses in a phrase, and later to engage in word and sentence play (e.g., thinking of a word or words that rhyme(s), "straightening" sentences—correcting word order, filling in missing parts of a sentence, etc.). During the first year or two, however, individual language play is generally the most rewarding to both infant and teacher.

LANGUAGE METHODS FOR EACH TYPE OF ACTIVITY

SOCIAL PLAY

Beyond the general aspects of interaction, each of the types of activity promotes special approaches to language stimulation. Social play centers attention on the communication value of language between caregiver and child, or, where more than one child is involved, on communication between children as well. This is in contrast to the functions of language in all other activities, in which language is directed principally toward the physical environment and relations between people and objects.

Social play takes a number of forms, the most informal of which are probably the little smiles, hugs, and pats that occur at odd moments during the day. These activities gradually develop into culturally prescribed rituals using language. Among these are "Peekaboo," nursery rhyme activities, personal dialogues, and such large movement activities as holding the infant up high, and gentle tickling or rolling. Activities with nursery rhymes represent language metaphorically in dramatic movements that physically involve the child. Such Anglo-Saxon classics as "Rock-a-Bye Baby," "This Little Pig Went to Market," "There Was a Little Mouse," and "Ride a Cock Horse" all have in common ritual movements that engage the child, sometimes with a surprise climax that children come to anticipate with excitement. One of the important elements of "Peekaboo" is the disappearance and reappearance of the caregiver (in the infant's view), giving the infant valuable experience in the idea of the permanence of things, in this case of social objects. All cultures, language and dialect communities have their own store of similar poetic activities for engaging children in this way. This is another reason why each group of more than two or three children in a center from an identifiable dialect group or culture should have access to caregivers familiar with the group's cultural lore.

Large movement activities may use less language, but they bring in kinesthetic experiences and close physical contact between people as a vital aspect of social relations. Personal dialogues start early with babbling, which as words and phrases are acquired, evolve into more complex forms of interpersonal communication between caregiver and child. Dialogues typically involve spontaneous expressions of mood and state, how the child is feeling at that time. As language develops, brief, shared comments on a just completed event, an ongoing activity or a plan for what to do become more and more part of a relationship between caregiver and child. Such practices, common in the personal relations of the family, can have their place in day care to the extent caregivers develop close and continuing relations with infants.

To avoid using the infant merely as a sounding board, make sure that the infant is actively participating. Watch closely for expressions of delight, along with vocalizing, babbling, or talking, according to age. The process should not be a lecture, but a form of interpersonal communication involving language.

Early in development (less than six months), infants respond primarily to the sound and patterns of a familiar voice, which gives them practice in the sound basis for language. Soon they begin to vocalize. As they begin to learn more about sound patterns, they string sounds together, that is they babble, which soon includes intonational expression. But even before infants start to approximate words, they begin to understand a word here and there in the adult's speech, which heightens their pleasure. The early limited interaction becomes more and more a true dialogue, culminating in infants contributing words and sentences to express complete ideas of their own.

This kind of social interaction is an important basis for developing intimacy in relations closely tied to language. Socially useful language appears extensively in the basic care routines, but the special focus on intimacy in social play, combined with experimentation with language forms at each successive stage, adds much to social development. As language becomes a well-mastered tool, the preschool child will enjoy further extension of this dialogue to the activities of social games. Simple *games with agreed upon rules,* such as passing a bean bag or ball, following a leader, taking turns walking a board, and eventually playing tag, lotto, and other more complex games, provide basic experience in social rules in which language plays a major role. Many social and other general concepts of taking turns, imitating others, ordering in time, social roles, multiple social interaction, leader-follower relations and reciprocity are learned through these group social games.

OBJECT PLAY

Stimulating language through object manipulative play teaches the child knowledge of language as a tool for describing and acting on the environment. The activity takes place immediately in front of the infant, using interesting small objects, which maximally engages his attention. Social play, care routines, and labeling trips, indoors or out, all tend to engage the child in language in relation to prescribed rituals. While the child's attention is similarly engaged in object play, the activity is less tied to a social ritual or a schedule of events. Objects can be played with at will, varying choice, number, and pace without schedule. Each feature and action that engages the child can often be labeled clearly several times in the course of a play session, taking care to stress the relevant term at the moment of focus (e.g., "touch the *knob,*" "*pull* the string"). Such flexibility helps the rules of language stand out more clearly. Moreover, language is less bound to set rituals. Objects and movements can be chosen and varied so as to demonstrate more of the language forms easiest for the infant to grasp and pronounce at each stage.

It is convenient to *prepare a kit* of five to fifteen objects placed on a shelf near the site where the language object play is routinely scheduled, or in a portable box if there is no set place. Two types of objects are usually included. One type, composed of a few blocks and containers, is employed as props to support the child's play. The second is a set of miniature replicas of objects that lend themselves to labeling, such as doll furniture and other household items, small figures of people and animals, vehicles, tools, and almost anything that can be found that represents culturally common objects.

Certain items, such as small bottles, eating utensils, and watches can be presented in full size. But it is important that all the items be small enough for the child to handle and see as a whole easily, since it is easier for the infant to learn their names and functions under such conditions. Well-defined features on replicas insure easier recognition.

Two or three examples of each type of object, such as two tables, two spoons, and two cars, are needed to help the infant grasp the fact that each word represents a *concept* of something, not just one object. Other parts of speech, such as verbs and prepositions, need the same sort of variation. When one makes a series of movements (e.g., "roll") to demonstrate an action term, or to show a relationship for a preposition (e.g., "on"), try to perform the movements in different ways and use several different objects. Qualifiers, that is adjectives describing characteristics of or relations between objects (e.g., "more," "blue," "small"), also require different examples (e.g., different objects painted various shades of blue and objects of different sizes), in order to teach language and concepts in a general way and not rote labeling. Adjectives and adverbs are more difficult concepts that come later, however. The order and frequency of presenting objects for language learning form part of the language sequences outlined further on.

PICTURE STORY, POETRY, AND ORAL LANGUAGE ACTIVITIES

Picture story activities bear many resemblances to learning language through play with objects, but differ mainly in the restriction of movement. Objects in pictures are pointed to and talked about but they are awkward to manipulate in play, except when cut out and pasted on cardboard. Their chief functions are to expand the child's ability to abstract and imagine, and portray numerous things and scenes clearly and frequently in a way impossible to duplicate in real life. Picture viewing and labeling may be started by the age of six months, offering single pictures of one clear object set in a plain, contrasting background of the type available in ABC books (but ignoring the letters). As the infant begins to show interest in pictures he/she will want to look at a series of pictures, some of which gradually show more complicated objects and background scenes. Well-defined pictures of objects cut out from magazines and pasted on plain white cardboard are an inexpensive source for extending the variety of pictured objects. It is important to recognize that several sessions of looking at pictures are usually needed before infants develop a definite interest, but that the interest will come very early when patience, persistence, and simple pictures are employed. The process is greatly aided by finding objects that look like the pictured objects and presenting the two side by side, alternately drawing attention to the picture and letting the infant handle the object. Balls, boxes, cars, keys, and lamps lend themselves to such comparisons because they have such distinctive features that make exact duplication of object and picture less important. Good color photographs of actual replicas and other objects also help.

Stories, rhymes, poems, and other printed text serve no purpose in the early stages; they only complicate the process beyond the infant's ability to understand. Usually after a few months of language activity with pictures, books with a few simple phrases and sentences may be introduced, the caregiver first reading only an occasional phrase, emphasizing a key word as the object or feature is pointed to (by the caregiver or child). Bit by bit, as the infant's interest and span of attention expands, more phrases can be brought in for each picture, until the infant enjoys following a few pages and eventually an entire story text, accompanied by pictures.

One of the secrets of enjoyable story reading is the manner of introducing each new picture story book. On initial reading, simply view a few pictures with the child, pointing out or responding to the child's interest by labeling and talking about an occasional pictured object. At first ignore the text entirely and cover only as many pictures as the infant shows interest in. Even many preschoolers, particularly those whose experience with books is limited, require this acclimatizing process to a new book. With each successive session, more pictures and items can be talked about, and the text itself referred to during the third or fourth session, usually first in simplified form, using the quality of the child's response as a guide.

Story and poetry reading lead naturally into *story telling* and *recitation of poetry,* that is purely *oral language activities.* Few adults of our time feel equipped to recite poetry or tell stories, but it is one of the more engaging techniques of developing children's interest in language and literature. In some ways these activities blend well into relaxed periods of social play and in fact there is no reason to always draw clear distinctions between stories and social play, other than to insure that both activities are well represented in every child's daily experience.

Oral language activities free the situation from the constraints of a book, allowing adult and child a more flexible relationship, in which each may observe and respond more closely to the other. Story telling is the more flexible, since, other than following a story line, the exact content and sequence of events can be varied considerably with each telling. Much of course depends on the imagination of the caregiver. Poems generally follow an exact form or lose much of their rhythm, imagery, and style, though small variations won't matter and are worth the value of the experience for the child. It is easier to watch the child's degree of responding and to vary one's tone accordingly while reciting than while reading.

Poetry recitation begins with infants in the short, ringing nursery rhymes of social play. The actions performed do much to maintain the child's interest. Stories begin with one or two sentence statements of simple actions (e.g., playing with a ball, washing hands, petting a dog), which gradually become expanded into stories with a beginning, a middle, and an end. Again, the performance of the actions by the child (or perhaps first by the caregiver, to get the infant going), will arouse interest. In either case, it is the *repeated use of the same rhymes or phrases* that enables the infant to say the phrases and recite the rhyme without apparent effort. In addition to contributing to the development of memory, the process develops the child's imagination and an entirely new means of literary expression of a rather informal, personal sort. As the infant begins to use language more and his attention span lengthens, phrases begin to become stories, in which imaginary characters encounter a series of events, and rhymes turn into longer poems with more complex imagery. The early stages (i.e., until about the preschool period) will find short poems with a concrete story line generally more appealing to most children, however. The child's involvement in gradually telling small parts of and eventually entire stories himself, or in reciting an occasional line and eventually all of a favorite poem, is a manageable goal for oral language activities. Involvement depends on the ease, informality and enjoyment with which the caregiver herself shares in the process. When the process goes well, the child will spontaneously begin to tell or recite. Pressing him to participate, on the other hand, may delay or even permanently inhibit his desire to express himself.

The caregiver's own skills and interest in story telling and reciting poetry will come best simply by doing them. Guidance or prior training are of course valuable, but trying out these activities daily will go far in making the process successful and interesting for caregivers. Reading the same poems and stories in which the child shows an interest over and over again will familiarize both child and adult to such a degree that soon the adult and eventually the child will find it easy to tell a story and recite a poem without the aid of the book. Much can also be learned through observing and talking with others.

Telling stories can also be based on children's everyday experiences or on things adults do that children daily observe and can understand. Simply string a few common actions together into a sequence leading up to a simple climax, like jumping in the water or seeing a huge bird. Stories about a birthday party, visiting a friend, going to a store, or going swimming make natural interest activities that will capture the child's attention. Nor do the characters need always be imaginary. Young children enjoy short stories in which a close playmate or even the child himself is the hero. Animal stories involving a pet, or forest, zoo, or farm animals are favorite themes for children.

LANGUAGE ON TRIPS (INDOORS AND OUTDOORS)

Labeling and narrating about things to be seen on *"trips,"* whether indoors or out, expands vocabulary and knowledge of new areas. Trips do not focus on language alone, of course, since most excursions serve many purposes, including fun and just traveling. But while an excursion to the waterfront, train depot, or even a neighborhood store is an expedition, short tours around a day care center kitchen, bathroom, or staff lounge, can easily concentrate on language, because the brief time expended (ten to fifteen minutes) raises no difficulty in scheduling a variety of other purposes on other occasions.

The methods of labeling and interacting for tours indoors, around a center are essentially the same as those for object labeling with a kit of replicas on the floor. The difference is the added pleasure the infant finds in moving around in company with a caregiver and the novelty of varied sights to scan and labels to learn. But repetition is still basic to the activity, taking repeated tours to the kitchen, for example, reviewing the familiar labels over a series of tours and limiting the number of terms reviewed or introduced on each occasion. It is useful to visit the same area several (e.g., four to five) times in a row, perhaps every other day or so before shifting to another area. A kitchen in particular offers many possibilities. About five to six review terms and two to three new terms are easily assimilated by infants under two and perhaps double the number for most children beyond two. Search and find games on these tours are special delights to children, particularly when in groups of twos and threes. The caregiver has only to name a familiar object, perhaps one recently introduced and only partially learned, and ask the child to find it. The same process will also work with familiar events, such as a cook washing dishes or a caregiver writing in the lounge.

Community excursions offer infinite possibilities for language and concept learning. It is only necessary to keep in mind the usual interaction techniques and to watch for opportune moments to label a scene that attracts a child. There is really little that is special about techniques for community trips, except that language is ordinarily employed more sparingly. The child's attention is naturally taken up with the task of moving from place to place and with drinking up the sights of novel scenes and events.

Certain of the standard techniques are particularly useful to increase the travel pleasure and language experience, indeed the entire experience, for the child. First of all, it is a mistake to always wait for the child to show interest in some aspect of each new scene before describing it. Without direction, young children usually lack the broad understanding needed even to notice the main things going on. We tend to notice (perceive) only what we understand, and the child's understanding can be greatly aided by pointing out and describing in simple ways the significant parts of unfamiliar activities. Such activities as buying and selling in stores, digging trenches to repair sewer pipes in streets or docking a large freighter are usually too unfamiliar and complex for the child to grasp until the caregiver draws attention to the exchange of money and goods, the action of the teeth of the machine shovel actually digging, and the throwing of the huge hawsers (ropes) to tie the ship. Spontaneity is important and overdirection is a risk, but spontaneity alone does not lead to development. Interest and understanding are interrelated; both will expand through a warm and guiding, but nonpushing relation with an adult who is herself/himself interested and involves the child through brief and simple explanations, timed to the activity in process.

The second thing is repetition of experience. Several visits to the same or very similar types of stores, building construction activities, and other settings make visits increasingly interesting and informative to the child. He/she soon acquires the main lines of what is happening to what and the names of key items and functions. The knowledge acquired makes him/her feel at home with the activity and interested in searching for additional details.

A third technique for adding to the child's pleasure and rate of understanding is coordinating visits with the theme play and story activities in day care. Reading picture story books and magazines about trains; making sets of trains and related materials specially available for floor play; furnishing conductor uniforms and related props for sociodramatic play; and encouraging train themes in art and craft activities multiply the children's interest in and ability to understand what is going on when they visit a railroad station or switching yards.

Most of the other techniques that are useful for developing language in object play and other settings apply with equal force to outings. Use language that is simple, concrete, and stated with enthusiasm and personal expression. Pick new things to label to fit each infant's progress and use single words or stressed words in a sentence timed to the event. Complete phrases and sentences are stimulating from the beginning, and simple, pointed explanations of how key features work (e.g., how the sharp bow of a ship enables it to cut the water) become increasingly valuable as language and understanding develop—but avoid preaching and strung out descriptions at all cost. Spontaneity and easy interaction between adult and child on excursions here, as everywhere, will make the difference between a chore and an adventure.

At what age should excursions begin? In some senses, it is never too early; by three to six months the sights and sounds of the wider world begin to broaden the infant's responses, making him/her better prepared at one year for still wider enjoyment. Practically speaking, day care centers will probably often rely on parents to make use of the daily travel between home and center to stimulate the child's language and concepts in relation to the community at large, particularly during infancy. One of the important routines for caregivers is to regularly discuss with parents the value of these activities and how to do them.

For the center excursion program, it is probably better to pass the child's first year in stroller rides and walks around the neighborhood, taking advantage of the traffic of people and vehicles, an occasional street construction or building project, and the convenience of a neighborhood store or gas station. A rich foundation vocabulary and much information can be learned through neighborhood strolls. Like basic care activities, they are—or ought to be—routine, steeping the infant in repeated experience with a diversity of concepts.

During the child's second year, neighborhood walks can be extended with benefit. They can last a little longer, provide more detail, and gradually embrace more complicated events. Trips to special stores, such as a supermarket or perhaps a shoe repair store, become more interesting, particularly when repeated on several occasions. By age two or more, depending on how much excursions and stimulation in general have been part of her/his daily fare, language is rapidly becoming well established as a meaningful tool and the child is likely to find excursions a most enriching part of her/his life.

I. LANGUAGE SOUND LEARNING (PHONOLOGY)

GENERAL CHARACTERISTICS OF SOUND STIMULATION ACTIVITY

1. The main activity consists of face-to-face, *vocal imitative play* with language sounds between caregiver and infant most often during social play activities. Imitative sound play is an excellent foundation for language, including the aesthetic aspects of language in both poetry and prose.
2. Use single vowels (V) and consonants (C) and consonant-vowel (CV) syllable combinations (e.g., pa, ti), singly and in series (e.g., pa-pa . . . , boo-la-di . . . , etc.).
3. Watch for spontaneous vocalizations of the infant—most likely to occur during social play and face-to-face relations in basic care routines (e.g., feeding solids, diaper changing, and dressing), but may also appear during object play and story reading. Respond with smiles and/or imitate vocalizations.
4. Demonstrate correct sounds and sound patterns. Express pleasure (e.g., smile, say "That's fine!") at infant's efforts to imitate; then repeat correct version two to three times, pausing slightly between each utterance. *Articulate clearly*—use lips (and tongue) and demonstrate when infant is attending.
5. Introduce only one or two units per session.
6. Review all sound units and patterns regularly, but covering only a few each session, which may last from one or two to fifteen or twenty minutes, depending on interest.
7. Imitative play may sometimes develop into repeated cycles of *imitative interaction,* caregiver and infant copying each other several times—often with laughter.
8. As evident from the highly overlapping time periods below, the sequence is highly flexible. Thus, for example, repetitive strings of familiar CV syllables and individual letter contrasts can be introduced almost from the

start. The main thing is to play with lots of sounds in a clear, but flexible and playful manner.

9. Vocal imitative play is often more fun when occasionally interspersed with other forms of social play.

Sequence of Sound Rules   *Added Points on Stimulation*

Levels and Starting Age (Months): I.   0–6+

1. Single vowel and consonant sounds.
2. Consonant-vowel (CV) syllable combinations (e.g., pa, po, pa, pe, pi, ta, ma, etc.).

1. Usually demonstrate no more than two to three single sounds (C or V) or syllables (CV) per session.

2. Use simpler *frontal consonants* (label *b*, *p*, and *m* and dentals, *d*, *t*, and *n*) and more *open vowels* (*a* as in ball and *o* as in dog) first, though *back consonants* (e.g., *c* as in cut, *g* as in go) and narrower vowels (*i* in in and *u* in up) can follow soon after.

3. Brief two to three minute sessions are preferrable in early stages.

Levels and Starting Age (Months): II.   3–8+

1. Contrast pairs of single C and V sounds (e.g., *b* versus *d* and *a* versus *i*).
2. Contrast pairs of CV syllable (e.g., ba versus pa, mo versus mi).

Once the infant has learned to attend and participate in vocal imitative play, sessions may be extended (five or more minutes) and a greater variety of units reviewed each session.

Levels and Starting Age (Months): III.   4–10+

1. Contrast pairs of VC syllables (e.g., ap, og, in, up, etc.).
2. Two syllable repetitions, (e.g., ba-ba, fo-fo, etc.).
3. Two syllable variations, (e.g., ba-po, ga-mi, og-bi, etc.).
4. Syllable strings, both repetitive series (e.g., ti-ti-ti-ti . . .) and varying strings (e.g., mo-gu-li . . .).

1. Continue also to use Level II units and syllables to extend the variety of individual C and V sounds and combinations. More complex sounds and patterns like sh, ch, st and bru versus tru can gradually be introduced.

2. Note that *actual words* can be employed in these sound games, without paying much attention to meaning in this activity.

Levels and Starting Age (Months): IV.   6–12+

1. Contrast pairs of CVC combinations, both actual words and nonsense words (e.g., cap versus tap, bog versus nog, etc.).
2. Strings of CVC actual and nonsense words.

1. Repetitive word strings (e.g., top-top-top-top . . .) or strings with variations (e.g., top-tip-tup, etc.), are both useful. Meaning is still ignored, that is for vocalization play, and it may be some weeks before the infant pronounces the final consonant.

2. With these units, imitative activities move gradually into *word play activities*, however, paralleling the infant's first awareness of words

Sequence of Sound Rules	*Added Points on Stimulation*

as words (whole language entities) that stand for (symbolize) things, as early as six to nine months for infants already stimulated (home or day care), but usually between ten and fourteen months. The infant begins to realize the fixed values of each word, which are fun to vary deliberately in play. Strings of words the infant knows, caregiver and infant imitating each other in series, can be followed by a variation, (e.g., dog-dog-dog-dig-dog). This can be done even before the infant pronounces the final consonant clearly. The infant comes to anticipate the insertion of the variant term (i.e., dig) with considerable excitement.

Levels and Starting Age (Months): V. 15–18 Through Preschool

1. Pairs of *complex rhyming words* (e.g., trip versus ship, tree versus three) or alterations (e.g., lip versus lap).
2. Other *word play units*, such as long, real and nonsense words, varying by only one or two letters (piggy-paggy), reversed words (e.g., bip-pib).
3. Phrase and sentence units.

1. Beginning as early as fifteen to eighteen months with advanced talkers (who begin phrases by this period), word play and its endless elaboration in rhyming and phrase/sentence manipulation offer many possibilities for perfecting pronunciation, understanding, and the literary-poetic possibilities with language, (even into the school years and adulthood).

2. Among the many variations and extensions are:

a. Speed, accuracy, the length of sound strings, variety of units in any string and in the infant's repertoire may increase rapidly by this period—depending on the quality and extent of prior language stimulation.
b. The infant may soon be able to correct the word version offered by the caregiver and eventually (eighteen to twenty-four months or later) to invent terms of her/his own. These skills emerge through the caregiver's deliberately mispronouncing (or omitting some sound in) a word that is highly familiar to the infant, who then will utter the correct pronunciation. Longer words (can be mispronounced as vocabulary expands e.g., caregiver: "hippopogamus"—infant: "hippopotamus"). As the child's skills advance, the caregiver can introduce more than one error into a word, the number depending on the length and familiarity of the word to the child.

c. *Phrase and sentence play offer* further extensions for rhyming and conflicts with correct forms. Completing sentences with rhyming words or deliberately substituted, misrhymed words, particularly in familiar nursery rhymes and poems; presenting an alliterative string of words (e.g., See Sally sit) for the child to imitate or add to; omitting final words (or words in other positions) for the child to think of a rhyming or alliterative word; and even simple spelling games are among activities increasingly appropriate and pleasurable for preschoolers to develop a more elaborate grasp and aesthetic appreciation of the sound structure of language.

II. WORD LEARNING (SYMBOLS-MORPHOLOGY-SEMANTIC-PARTS OF SPEECH)

GENERAL CHARACTERISTICS OF WORD LEARNING ACTIVITIES

1. Here, the main activity moves from face-to-face, vocal interaction to *naming (labeling) things* (object-referent relations). This activity is the key basis for learning language as an abstract tool, a set of symbols for representing the world, and for communicating ideas. Word learning activities should *parallel sound stimulation activities,* following the schedule outlined below.

2. Labeling objects *is most effective when done in the course of caregiver-infant interaction* in cooperative play (object manipulation, social play, and picture viewing), in basic care routines or on excursions.

3. The process is one of a caregiver applying an appropriate word, commonly employed to refer to some object, at the moment the caregiver (or the infant) touches (or points to, handles, etc.), the item named. *Timing* is essential, that is, to point and label close to the same instant.

4. *Words refer to all kinds of things,* including objects, actions, features of objects, relations between things, etc., for which we use nouns, verbs, adjectives, prepositions, etc., (*parts of speech*), respectively, to label the different things.

5. A word is not simply a name for a particular object (or action, feature, etc.), however, but is an abstract term (symbols) we apply to *all* objects (or actions, etc.), having similar characteristics. Thus, the infant needs *several examples for each new word* introduced, each example varying slightly in nonessential characteristics. For instance, when a *ball*

is first named, be sure that the word is applied to at least one other ball of a different color, size, and/or material during the first or second exposure and additional, somewhat different balls in subsequent days. Balls are all alike in that they are round and roll, but many vary considerably in other features having nothing to do with being a ball. Different examples are necessary for the infant to develop a broad, flexible grasp of language, and not simply a narrow, rote use of it.

It is evident that word learning is *dependent on concept learning,* in which the child progresses according to how well she/he is stimulated in guided learning activities and the richness of everyday experience. But language activities themselves will contribute much to foster the child's development of concepts. Becoming aware that each noun stands for a *type* of thing, each verb for a *type* of action, and especially that modifiers represent *all* instances of an attribute of an object, for example, dark, fuzzy, or purple, is at the very basis of learning concepts. Language and concept (knowledge) learning programs therefore complement one another.

6. Since language is obviously complex and cannot be learned all at once, it will help infants to learn by *simplifying* the terms used and *following a certain order,* an order based more or less on the natural order of difficulty of language rules. As will be outlined below, the sequence begins by concentrating on *simple nouns and verbs* that represent *small, familiar objects* and *easily visible movements,* leaving more difficult forms like adjectives and adverbs until later. Labels are often used alone, but also frequently when used in sentences, in which cases the *relevant word is stressed* (again, timing the stress with pointing to the item labeled).

7. Naming things *close to and immediately in front of the infant* helps him to see and understand better. The infant becomes more involved, particularly when he can *handle the thing himself,* or when some dramatic movement is performed, such as a quick movement with the object labeled or hiding it, making a noise, etc. For this reason, action words or at least process terms (e.g., up, down) are sometimes easier to learn because, even though a movement is only temporary (unlike a solid object), a movement holds the infant's attention, which is essential for learning.

8. Although simplifying is important through initially selecting and stressing easy words, experience in hearing *naturalness of expression* is also important. The infant needs to hear a lot of complete sentences said in a natural tone of voice in order to grasp the full range of sound patterns of the language (e.g., rhythm, intonation, pitch). Using words in sentences also gradually helps to clarify meanings difficult to express in single words, as discussed below in the sentence learning curriculum. Ordinary conversation in the infant's presence, as well as interpersonal monologues in social play and easy "conversation" addressed to the infant in care routines serve these purposes very well. Key words may still be stressed and related to objects and events, but they are embedded in actual sentences.

9. *Frequency* and *variety* are additional keys to insuring the rich develop-

ment of language. *Many brief (two to five minutes) labeling sessions spread throughout the day* are more productive and often easier to manage than two or three prolonged sessions, though an occasional longer session will lead to exploration of variations in language and personal relations that may otherwise be missed. The easiest way to accomplish these goals is build them into a *daily cycle* of care routines and other activities.

10. *Review* new words over a number of days and old words regularly as practicable, being sure not to make a drill out of it. Keep things varied, flexible, and playful.

11. Remember that *understanding words comes before speech* (sometimes by several months). *Watch for behavioral signs of understanding* (e.g., the infant clearly looking at or touching the right object, when several are present, the infant performing an action verbally requested—but not performed—by the caregiver; and the infant turning toward, or showing pleasure and anticipation when a key word is mentioned, like milk, bottle, cookies, juice, up—meaning to be picked up). Patience and persistence in language stimulation will be rewarded by words—one or two at a time—coming earlier.

12. *The age ranges for starting* each "*level*" in the sequence below are *very broad,* because infants enter day care at many different ages and stages of language development. So much depends on how much *effective* attention to language the infant has already received. The *levels are also approximate,* as for other types of concept learning. As long as the approach is play oriented and flexible with some thought devoted to simplifying the labeling process and choice of words, levels can overlap considerably.

13. Many of the *infant's first words take on meanings different from common adult* usage. Infants' first words are likely to be rather vague and overgeneralized (e.g., all footwear are shoes) or limited to the particular object she knows (e.g., her own bottle). Moreover, there tend to be *just two general categories, things,* and *actions* (or processes). The former include static states or events (e.g., hot-cold, all gone, done, here, and that), and the latter include social action linked expressions and processes (e.g., bye-bye, peekaboo and thank you) and certain adverbs/prepositions (e.g., up-down and on-off) that are used to indicate a total process of personal experience (e.g., a request to be set down on the floor or to get off the potty).

   Even things and actions do not maintain clear distinctions. Thus adjectives, such as hot, nice, pretty, good, bad, etc., adverbs, such as no-yes, here-there, etc., and even prepositions, such as up, off, etc., first usually mean *both* some state (thus a thing—noun) or even a place (e.g., on) *and* a personal process (e.g., good = I am a good girl; no = I don't want to do something; and off = take my hat off). Depending on the extent and precision with which the forms of speech are used by caregivers and on the quality of her general concept stimulation, the infant soon begins to understand and use speech in less personalized and more objective, differentiated forms, (e.g., to refer to an object as *big, wet,* or *there* simply as a descriptive fact that interests her, rather than necessarily because she wants something, or to ask *what,* because she wants to know the name of an unfamiliar object, not just because she wants it).

14. The relatively *more abstract speech forms* (like adjectives, adverbs, etc.) are easier for the child to learn through *showing contrasts,* using objects whose name the child already knows. For example, present one red ball and one blue (green, yellow, etc.) ball, side by side or one big bear and one small bear (both toys), in each case pointing to the object to which the modifier applied (i.e., "red" for "big" object); or move a toy car alternately "fast" and "slowly," labeling appropriately.

15. The words of the more *abstract parts of speech,* especially pronouns, and verb tenses (i.e., past, future, etc.), are usually *easier to learn in relation to other words in sentences,* in which a set of relationships are described. For the young child, the adjective "red" is applied (as in the examples above) to some particular red object ("a red truck") or the adverb "fast" to the speed of some car ("the car is moving fast"). She/he has no abstract ideas of color or speed. Similarly, when a caregiver says *"I give the cup to you,"* the sentence context furthers the understanding. Much complex word learning in short will come through using words in sentences which should be widely employed (as described in the next section on sentence learning). Nevertheless, it is also essential for the infant to understand a particular relation to which a term applies, by applying such abstract terms alone in contrast pairs (without always using phrase relations); or for pronouns, especially, performing the actions that illuminate the relations, while saying the sentence. But variation in word forms that come with verb tenses, (especially, those using compound forms like "will go"), comparisons of adjectives, (e.g., big, bigger, biggest) and plurals inevitably require much sentence use to understand.

Sequence of Word Learning Rules	*Added Points on Stimulation*
Levels and Starting Age (Months): I. 0–10+	
1. Concrete objects (nouns) 2. Simple actions (verbs)	1. *Objects (nouns).* Use mostly small, familiar objects the infant can handle. *Avoid pronouns.* Repeat the same noun for the same and similar objects each time they are indicated. 2. *Actions (verbs).* Begin with the most literal and visible types of actions, such as touch, pull-push, smile, kiss, hug, sit, stand, walk (depending on age). 3. During the first few months, until manipulative skills become more developed and coordinated, present objects and perform actions that are labeled in: a. visual following activities

Sequence of Word Learning Rules　　　　*Added Points on Stimulation*

b. placing objects in the infant's grasp to touch (label when he/she touches or holds)

c. helping her/him to both see and touch (handle) the object that is labeled.

4. *Language skills acquired*: No word understanding—only sound and variation discrimination. No speech—only increasingly accurate vocalization and imitation of language sounds.

Levels and Starting Ages (Months): II.　6–18+

1. Concrete objects (nouns) and movements (verbs) as above.

2. Repertoire of nouns gradually expands and may include some larger objects (e.g., door) that interest the infant.

3. Action terms will similarly expand in number and may begin to include a variety of social *experience related terms* (e.g., up-down, bye-bye, hi, peekaboo, etc.).

1. As manipulative skills develop, broaden visual following and placement-to-grasp, labeling activities to engage the infant's own manipulations, and to vary the angles and distances involved.

2. Expect to label more frequently the objects with which the infant spontaneously plays (from the set of word learning objects placed before her/him); as well as the *actions* she/he makes spontaneously (or in imitation of the caregiver). Be sure to *time the naming* with the infant's attention to the object, or the movement, and be sure it is a clear movement that lends itself to naming (such as hold, or drop, pick up, touch, open-close, etc.).

3. *Continue to minimize pronouns*, repeating the object name each time.

4. *Language skill acquired.*
Understanding: First words understood are the labels of highly familiar objects tied to specific situations (i.e., words like ma-ma, bottle), understood only when a particular object is seen. Over a few weeks or longer, depending on experience, words gradually generalize to other situations and similar objects, and will arouse interest even when relevant objects are not present. Words may greatly overgeneralize (e.g., all vehicles become cars) or undergeneralize (e.g., only a favorite stuffed animal is called bear). Similarly, the number of words understood will begin to expand rapidly.
Speech. Babbling increases in length and variety of sounds in sound strings, until intonation patterns sound like real speech. The infant's imitations at some point begin to resemble single syllable words with the final consonant left off (e.g., ball = ba), and soon two syllable strings, e.g., "ma-ma" and "bye-bye," in which understanding expands as above. Spontaneous use of these first words may occur almost immediately or be

Sequence of Word Learning Rules   *Added Points on Stimulation*

delayed for months, again depending on experience. *Note* that involvement in learning to stand and walk will *not* necessarily delay speech development—unless caregiver stimulation and expectations for progress in language drop off.

Levels and Starting Ages (Months): III.   12–24+

1. Expanding repertoire of object (noun) and action (verb) labels and experiences (e.g., oh!, thank you, etc.).

2. *Object description terms* (e.g., hot, cool, rough, etc.) and *relational terms* (e.g., more, big, little, long, etc.)—both technically adjectives but apparently thought of as states or "things" by the child.

3. *Demonstrative terms* (e.g., this-that, the) and question terms (e.g., what, what's that?) (pronoun-adjective forms).

4. *Placement terms* (e.g., here-there and where-where is _____?)— (adverbial forms).

5. *Positive-negative* (i.e., yes-no).

1. Continue same forms of labeling in interactive play in all types of activity, but gradually elaborating the *imaginary sociodramatic and problem solving forms of play* as the infants symbolizing and language skills expand, especially during the second year.

2. *Introduce the various* descriptive, relational, and similar, more *abstract terms sparingly*, until the infant shows a definite awareness of the meaning of words and begins to increase her/his rate of word learning (beyond three to four words).

3. *Demonstrate carefully the meaning of these more difficult terms*, from time to time, as well as using them casually as labels at well-timed moments in activity. For example, "hot" is easier for the infant to understand if he comes alternately near something hot and cold, back and forth. (Obviously, be careful of touching things too hot; for this reason, the terms warm and cool or cold may be safer and therefore easier to teach first.) Or demonstrate "that" by pointing to two or three objects, one at a time, *not* pointing to one or two others. For example, say, "give me that and that" pointing to two things and leaving the others untouched). In this way, infants will be helped to understand more accurately the *uses* of these terms, rather than simply understanding them vaguely as "states."

4. *Introduce only one such term at a time*, (e.g., avoid using "this" until the infant responds correctly to "that," or can use "that" appropriately. At an early point, however, contrasts become useful, as for example demonstrating the difference between "this" and "that." The imperative "No!" rarely needs any special attention. Life's ordinary rules make it one of the first words for many infants. Naturally, various difficult words will be employed in ordinary speech around the infant, but try to minimize their use, or use them carefully as suggested.

5. *Use only the relatively more concrete form of these terms*, terms that provide obvious evidence. For ex-

Sequence of Word Learning Rules	*Added Points on Stimulation*

ample, a long, narrow stick is easy to see as long, simply in relation to everything else around it, but a short stick needs to be compared with a long one to see what short means (so postpone the word short until later).

6. *Note again that most relational-descriptive and other difficult forms come mainly with phrase and sentence learning,* since they necessarily apply to a series of events and relations, as will be discussed in the next section on sentence learning.

Levels and Starting Age (Months): IV.   15–36+

1. Expanding repertoire of above descriptive-relational terms:
Articles (the; a-an, later)
Adjectives (e.g., short, tall, wide, slow; colors, numbers one to five).
Adverbs (e.g., fast, slowly; not, don't).
2. *Prepositions* (e.g., on-off, in-out, under-beside, etc.).
3. *Pronouns* (e.g., it, my, your, he, she, I, you, me).
4. *Conjunctions* (e.g., and, or).
5. *Plurals of nouns* (e.g., book-books; man-men).
6. *Verb tenses* (e.g., ask-asked; go-went).
7. *Comparisons of size (magnitude)* (e.g., small-smaller; loud-louder; good-better).

1. Continue to demonstrate and introduce carefully and slowly the various descriptive-relational terms.

2. Again, continue to introduce the new abstract terms, such as prepositions slowly and carefully. It may be helpful to follow the order indicated in the examples in the sequence of units. For example, introduce the article "the" before "a" and "an," and the pronoun "it," then "my" and "your" (all of which are easier to point out externally to the child), followed by "he" and "she." More difficult conjunctions, such as "because" and "since," the pronouns "I," "your," "me," and "they," and other increasingly complex and abstract forms of all parts of speech, will come later (past eighteen to twenty-four months) and probably take much time to learn and necessarily demand much sentence activity. The many irregular verb forms, nouns, plurals, etc., in particular, can only develop through long and constant example of others and by experimentation on the part of the child. For example, young children often first extend the regular past tense form of verbs to irregular forms (e.g., bought = "buyed"). Many verb forms, moreover, are compound word combinations, e.g., "will have," "have gone," necessarily based on sentence development.

III. PHRASE-SENTENCE LEARNING (SYNTAX-MORPHOLOGY-SEMANTICS)

GENERAL CHARACTERISTICS OF SENTENCE LEARNING ACTIVITY

1. Until the child learns to understand and use words in sentences language is incomplete. Almost everything we see and do has complicated mean-

ings that can only be fully expressed in sentences. Single words by themselves can only express vague and partial meanings or the names of things, without expressing purposes, processes, or relations between things. The essence of sentence activity is ordering words according to rules in order to describe and communicate interrelations between the means and ends and characteristics of things.

2. The rules for combining words into *sentences are learned through many activities:*

    a. Especially useful are the *sound and word learning activities, in which phrases and sentences are employed,* the key sound patterns and words being stressed by the tone of voice. These activities build language rules and word meanings that express the connection between things, as for instance, in the word "round" as a feature of a certain block, expressed in the phrase, "A round block"; or the word "roll" describing what a caregiver does with a ball, expressed in the sentence, "Roll the ball."

    b. The child also acquires much knowledge about sentence rules *through ordinary conversation* people conduct in her/his presence. Whether complicated or simple, occasional or frequent, at some distance or close by, the infant is half involved or simply present, the infant is exposed to examples of sentence making. The simpler and closer the conversation and the more the conversation is directed to the child and her/his immediate situation, the more the infant can grasp, even through no special effort is made to stress key words or relate labels to events.

    c. (Picture) *story reading* and *story telling activities,* in which forming sentences about things is the heart of the process. A special advantage of stories is the fact that stories follow a theme, in which ideas about a topic are developed through a series of sentences. Stories are thus valuable for expanding the child's understanding of language rules in a larger structure of interrelated meanings.

    d. *Poetry* too gives experience in sentence learning, providing a similar expansion of meaning through themes. But poetry gives more experience of a different kind, the expansion of language rules in metaphor, rhyme, and meter. The child learns how to use the parts of speech to form sentences in rich, subtle, and fanciful expressions of meaning, as well as gaining the experience described for acquiring the sound basis of language. Both stories and poems are also important aesthetic activities.

    e. A considerable portion of *sentence learning is derived from guided learning in concept curriculum programs* (including excursions). Much of the activity necessarily involves talking about concepts, in some ways similar to how word learning at the more advanced stages occurs: the difference is that complete sentences may be more frequent and the focus is on the concept, rather than on the language forms and rules. Size differences in concept learning, for example, in-

volve comparing many types of objects varying by size, the teacher
giving instructions as the differences are demonstrated by the teacher
and experimented with by the child. In word rule learning, on the
other hand, while size (or other concept) differences are often demonstrated, the attention of the child is directed more toward the word
forms (i.e., adjectives) used to indicate size comparisons, as, for example, wide, wider, and widest. As the child's language and cognitive
skills advance, these forms are eventually compared with other series,
such as short, shorter, and shortest, and tall, taller, and tallest, thus
establishing the general basis of the *language* rule for comparisons of
degree. Cognitive learning about size differences is of course also
taking place, but language rules are the focus.

Thus guided concept learning brings in much incidental exposure to
language forms through instruction and general talk about the learning and play.

f. Similar to the use of language in guided learning is the use of *language in basic care routines, excursions,* and any of the *other caregiving activities* in day care. Sometimes directed at language rules
and/or concept learning, but often as much a means of guiding the
child and accomplishing the task, much exposure to various sentence
rules occurs through these activities.

g. Sentence learning itself, a natural extension of word learning activities,
is directed at teaching grammatical rules of both the parts of speech
and sentence structure, through experimentation in making sentences.
Although any exposure to sentences in the various activities listed
above often teaches children something about these rules, playing with
sentences as such naturally provides the clearest method for learning about sentence structure and its relation to meaning, and expands
the child's knowledge of rules for the parts of speech.

The general sequence for learning sentence (syntactical) rules as outlined below is designed especially for planned activities in sentence
rule play. A certain amount of this type of play is also useful and
easy to use informally in other activities, such as caregiving routines
and reading/telling stories.

3. *Techniques for teaching sentence rules* essentially take *two forms:*

a. The most important is through *example* (modeling). The child learns
the cognitive rules for how sentences are made best simply through
learning *several examples of the rule,* from which she/he can grasp
the general idea about relations. For instance, a caregiver teaches the
rule about adjectives modifying nouns by saying expressions like "big
ball" and "wet hands." *Many examples* are often needed, because language rules are complicated and abstract, which is partly why it takes
many children several months between saying their first words and
making sentences: special attention to language helps the process.

b. The second form is to *guide the child's own efforts* to make sentences,
that is *to provide her/him with information on the accuracy of her*

phrase or sentence in terms of a rule (to provide feedback). It is more useful to the child to be given information on how her sentence may be improved than to simply say she is wrong. For example, if the child says, "Harry no go," the caregiver can say "Harry is not going," or "Harry did not go," depending on the context and the child's apparent meaning. In this way the teacher provides a correct example of relevant rules by improving (expanding) the child's version. This technique is a kind of *remodeling,* similar to the basic modeling technique.

4. There are of course many variations in how these techniques can be employed, but *simplifying sentences is especially helpful.* It is, for example, useful to *illustrate one rule at a time, using simple phrases,* instead of always using complete sentences. The rule (e.g., prepositions beginning a phrase) becomes more evident when several phrase examples, like "on the table," "under the table," and "beside the table," are used in place of complete sentences, such as "The toy is on the table," etc. Plenty of complete sentences appear in the other situations described; they may also be used here, but preferrably after illustrating the rule in isolated phrases, and more frequently as the child's general mastery becomes more fluent, usually between two to four years of age.

    It is evident that to illustrate single rules, one must either leave out words and word forms normally used, or stress only the key words and elements in a phrase. Using a phrase without a complete sentence may sound awkward to adults, but it will simplify the process for the child by having the rule stand out. In the phrases, "in (the) box" and "(the) cat (run)(s)," it is probably less awkward to say the entire phrase, merely stressing *in* and *box* and *cat* and *run,* than not to say the other elements at all. As in word learning, when more complete phrase-sentence forms are used expression is more natural, the correct model is provided, but only the key elements are drawn to the child's attention (by accenting and pointing) to avoid confusing her/him with more than one rule at a time.

5. Sentence rules are generally easier for young children to learn when the *examples are used with physical demonstrations* that illustrate meaning. Thus, the pivot terms of, e.g., the comparative form, "more water," "more marbles," and "more sand," become more meaningful to the child when water, marbles, and sand are actually added as the respective phrases are uttered. Many *picture books* and *magazine pictures* also display events and relations quite well. As has been noted they frequently depict with clarity scenes that are difficult to illustrate in the ordinary day care setting, such as a squirrel climbing a tree or smoke coming from a chimney, providing opportunity for greater variety in sentence making (e.g., "the squirrel climbs the tree," "smoke coming from the chimney").

6. *Contrasts.* As in word learning, or any concept learning, rules are clarified by presenting two examples of phrases in succession, showing the child the meaning as each example is alternately presented. For example,

say "on the can," "in the can," placing a toy appropriately with each utterance. As the child learns new words, more and more examples can be
used (e.g., in, on, under, beside). Moreover, vary the type of object
placed and the type of container to keep the play exciting. Be sure to involve the child in the activity, asking her/him to make demonstrations
and say the phrases to increase interest and deepen understanding.

7. *Avoid formal explanations about sentence rules.* The child needs to
understand and use language functionally through *using the rules.* She/
he does not need to be able to memorize or even say the rules, which is a
more difficult and abstract task.

8. *Use object manipulative* and *dramatic play* to enliven the learning of
phrase and sentence rules.

   In addition, as in the play with sounds, and words, *sentence rules
can be manipulated in verbal play,* for those rules about which the child
feels reasonably sure. For example, prepositional phrases or verb tenses
can be deliberately misstated, saying "the on floor" (using incorrect
order), "Suzie is drinking juice," after she finishes (wrong tense), or "the
girl which jumped" (instead of who). These activities involve certain
social task rules for how to play, which take a few sessions for many
children to learn. But by starting with obvious errors (e.g., "cookie
more" or "apple the") most children, beginning between two and one-
half to four, will enjoy this form of play immensely. *The key* is choosing
rules known to be fairly well mastered by a child. This type of play
consolidates and extends mastery of sentence rules and develops awareness of the utility of language rules, making it easier for children to learn
more rules.

9. Play with *phrase and sentence rules lends itself to group games* with several children, because no complicated learning materials are needed and
the play can be started almost anywhere at odd moments to enliven
otherwise dull periods (e.g., riding in a car, waiting in line, waiting for
meals, etc.). In such instances, it is unimportant that every child master
a given rule, as long as the correct rule is clearly illustrated and one or
two children and/or the caregiver agree on certain rules as in the case
of regional, dialectical, or colloquial differences. Whatever the day care
center policy with respect to "standard" language forms, make clear that
there are different ways of saying things. One can suggest, for example,
that people often/sometimes say, "I be," but that for this game it will be
easier if everyone says "I am." Be careful not to put down a particular
form or patronize the children.

10. Starting age ranges listed below are again very broad and levels flexible,
as for word learning. Norms are not established and children typically
learn in spurts and in many different ways. *Many sentence rules are
learned across broad, overlapping periods* as attention is turned alternately to different rules, according to experience and the problems the
rules present. Thus mastery for each rule runs through a cycle of crude
understanding to mastery and extension to new forms, a process that in-

volves constant interaction among rules being learned, and which extends over months and even years. Most basic sentence rules are learned in parallel between ages one and four, to different degrees of mastery.

11. It is evident that learning *phrase and sentence rules is closely tied with learning word rules* for the different parts of speech. For example, while it is useful to illustrate nouns and verbs separately, teaching the noun "ball" through pointing to various balls, and teaching the verb "roll," by rolling a ball (and other round objects), at some point the child will need to know how to combine the nouns and verbs ("ball" and "roll") to form a basic phrase form, such as "ball rolls" to describe the activity more completely. (The addition to the "s" for third person singular need not be drawn to the child's attention initially, as noted in point No. 4). Each type of learning, that is word meaning and sentence rules, is nevertheless useful to teach separately, teaching word meaning before combining words into sentences. But phrase-making activities closely follow and often overlap in time the individual word learning activities. Obviously, using phrases and sometimes complete sentences in word learning, in which key words are stressed, prepares the child for phrase-sentence learning.

12. The characteristics (criteria) that define levels in sentence learning are first of all the length (number of words) of the phrase/sentence. This factor is the most reliable overall measure of the child's development of language competence and furnishes a useful guideline for gradually expanding the number of rules for the child to cope with in each expression. Phrase length is the obvious major index of complexity for children because it reflects the number of new units the child can hold in his/her working memory, and because the number of relationships they must mentally keep track of in a sentence expands rapidly with the number of words in the sentence. Thus, for an expression containing only a single word, the infant need keep in mind only the single unit and its relation to meaning, that is, to the object or process it stands for (symbolizes). But to understand or use two words she/he must relate the two words to each other, as well as each word to what it stands for, *and* how the things referred to relate to one another, making a total of four relations. In the case of three words, the number of relations involve jumps to as many as nine, and for four word sentences to sixteen. This rapid expansion of the complexity of relations, which does not even account for how meaning and the complexity of synthesizing multiplies with increases in number, the child must handle is illustrated in two examples shown in Table 3–1.

There are three levels in the sequence defined in this way by phrase length, two-word combinations, three-word phrases and phrase-sentence units of four or more words. By the time the child first manages to grasp and use the number of relations in a four-word sentence, she/he is well into the problems of learning multiple combinatory rules for sentence construction (e.g., joining phrases, phrase expansion, embedding clauses) and the number of words makes relatively little difference. In some ways

TABLE 3–1. *Illustrations of Expansion of Number of Relations the Child Must Attend to with Increases in Phrase/Sentence Length.*

Type of Phrase/ Sentence	Language-Meaning Relations	Number of Words in Phrase/Sentence			
		One	Two	Three	Four
1. Noun to Noun Phrase	Language Form	table	on table	on the table	on the high table
	Meaning: Things referred to (referents)	object	location ↔ object	location ↔ specificity ↔ object	location ↔ specificity ↔ size relation ↔ object
2. Verb to Sentence	Language Form	drink	baby drink(s)	the baby drinks	the baby drinks milk
	Meaning: Things referred to (referents)	action	actor ↔ action	specificity ↔ actor ↔ action	specificity ↔ actor ↔ action ↔ object

the problem of holding units in mind becomes simplified, because sub-phrases of two and three units (e.g., "the cat" and "the black cat" are treated as modules, that is, they become units themselves that are manipulated in relatively automatic ways.

Within this basic framework of complexity levels, the child gradually advances in understanding *rules for employing different parts of speech in phrases and sentences.* Each of these rules must of course be learned in two ways: in terms of meaning (how words stand for things) and in terms of relations in a sentence, as diagrammed in the illustrations in Table 3–1. Suggestions for helping the child learn the first set of rules have already been outlined in the word learning curriculum. How words are related to make phrases and sentences is shown in terms of the three major levels of sentence length. By the time the child reaches the point of readiness to combine words into two-word combinations, that is after the infant has acquired a vocabulary of approximately twenty words (as my research has shown), the infant will already have begun to understand the meaning of many parts of speech, for instance, that certain words (nouns) stand for objects, that others (verbs) stand for processes, and still others (prepositions) refer to locational relations. The main problem then is to help her/him begin to understand words in combination, while continuing to relate words to actual things and relations. Each of the three levels in the sequence below provide illustrations for how the different parts of speech combine into phrases in different ways. At Levels II and III, however, additional rules for sentence construction, such as phrase joining, verb tense, and embedding phrases begin to appear, and some of these involve only two-word phrases.

It should be noted that caregivers can often use complete phrases and even sentences in guiding the child's sentence learning, just as in word learning. To simplify the examples for the child, simply *stress key words, stressing the number appropriate to the level the child has reached.* Thus at Level II, stress only two words, at Level III, three words, and so on. In this way, the number of relations the child has to attend to is kept within the learning level she/he can handle.

13. There are additionally *a number of general rules about language* and sentences the *child will learn with very little special attention,* simply by being exposed to words in phrase combination. Among these are *substitution* and *word order.* The former comes simply by the child learning that if one noun can represent an object, nouns always stand for objects (or entity at more abstract levels). The latter is learned by being exposed to a (relatively) constant word order (or arrangement of positions) for the respective parts of speech. More complex stages of these basic general rules, such as grasping the idea of a string of words (e.g., under the rug) substituting for a single word (noun) (as a module in certain positions), and how different parts of speech relate in specific ways and sequences, similarly are built into the process of teaching sentence rules, as shown in the following illustrations.

Sequence of Sentence Rules   *Added Points on Stimulation*

Levels and Starting Ages (Months): I.   12–18+

Two Word Combinations
(Basic Phrase Forms)

1. Noun-verb relations

a. Agent-action, e.g.,
(the) boy walk(s)
(the) boat sail(s)
b. Action-object, e.g.,
see (the) dog
give (the) doll (a cookie)

2. Simple modifiers

a. Characteristics, relations, or states
about objects (adjectives modifying
nouns), e.g.,
(1) red, one, little, another, more, etc.
apple(s) (or any appropriate noun).
(2) tree (is) green, big, wet, etc.
b. Indicating objects (demonstrative
adjectives or articles modifying nouns)
this tree, that cow, a book, an egg
(any object), the cap (specific object)
c. Possession and objects (pronouns-
nouns), e.g.,
my, your, her, his, their toy (boat,
shirt, etc.).
d. Characteristics of action (modifying verbs by adverbs), e.g.,
roll fast, slowly; climb up, down.

3. Relations of place or location
(prepositional phrases; place adverbs)

a. Subject location (noun-noun
phrase/adverb), e.g.,
(the book is) on (the) table . . . in
(the) box or, on/in here/there.
b. Action location (verb-noun
phrase/adverb, e.g.,
(walk) to (the) door . . . from
(the) kitchen or, to/from here/there.

4. Negatives

a. Nonexistence or absence, e.g.,

1. *Use complete phrases* (or sentences, as appropriate),
but stress only two key words at this beginning phrase
level, as discussed above.

2. *Frequently accompany phrases with demonstrations*
to teach meaning: For example, as each key word is
pronounced, point to the thing named (e.g., toy figure
of a boy or doll) or otherwise make the appropriate
movements (e.g., simulating walking with a toy figure).

Demonstrations with modifiers (e.g., adjectives indicating color, size, etc.), prepositions, negatives, and
other abstract relational terms are often learned more
easily by *showing contrasting relations* with contrasting
terms, as noted in the word learning curriculum.

Prepositions and pronouns work the same way, e.g.,
place a toy alternately "on" and "under" a chair while
saying the key term; or "your" hat and "her" hat,
while pointing to the appropriate hats.

3. At the two-word stage, the *child's expressions are
necessarily limited* and often quite varied from adult
language forms. A good number may consist of so-called
"pivot" terms, in which a generalized functional term
acts on or (modifies) an alternating variety of equiva-
lent terms, substituted for one another according to the
situation. Thus, in the expressions "more book" or
"more soup," and "eat cake," and "eat grape," the first
term is always a pivot around which many names of
things (nouns) or other characteristics (even adjectives) can be substituted according to need.
Two of the most basic types of sentence rules are
mastered in this process, how words relate to (modify)
one another and how words can substitute for one
another according to type and position.

4. The *main task for caregivers* is to *provide a rich
variety* of simple, useful phrases that include many of
the different parts of speech, as shown in the rule
sequence list in the column to the left. *Where a child
is unfamiliar with a particular part of speech*, it is
helpful to isolate examples of the form (e.g., adjectives
like rough, square, big) as in the word learning sequence. Thus the *word learning sequence continues for
many years* after sentence learning begins. While the

Sequence of Sentence Rules

no, no more (sand), all gone, mama (has) go(ne) away, daddy (is) away, light (is) gone; Paul (has) nothing.
b. Rejecting, prohibiting, e.g., don't shout; (the cat) can't go; (the baby wants) no more soup, milk, etc.
c. Denial (something is not so), e.g., (it's) not raining; (that) (is) not (a) bear.

5. Questions (interrogatives)

a. Identification and location of things, e.g.,
what's this, that?
where's (the) ball?
(who, when, and other wh_____ questions come later).

Added Points on Stimulation

complexities of abstract terms can only be fully understood in relation to other terms (and object-process relations), part of the process is also rooted in the particular function specific parts of speech perform (e.g., pronouns referring to persons and adjectives referring to features).

Word combinations therefore build on how well the word learning has progressed, that is according to the number of parts of speech with which the child has beginning familiarity. The child can combine into phrases only those parts of speech with which she/he has some understanding.

5. It will be noted that as in word learning many different parts of speech are represented at this level. Again this gives the child experience in many possible word combinations, developing her/his language competence broadly as well as complexly through learning sentences.

6. While there is *little need to correct these "telegraphic" or simplified pivot expressions*, it helps the child to keep using and demonstrating through action, various more correct, complete forms. Many of these pivot expressions are partially correct, moreover, (e.g., "little crayon," "go kitchen"), merely being incomplete. They show the child's efforts to deal correctly with phrase relations, but since she can handle only two word combinations, they are generally incomplete. Again, for this reason use complete phrase expressions, but stress two of the several words in a phrase to enrich her understanding at the level she is working on.

Levels and Starting Ages (Months): II.   16–30+

Three Word Phrase Combinations

1. Use all of the *basic phrase forms* used in Level I, but *stress three key words* and accompanying meanings, e.g., the ball rolls, this square block, walk to (the) door, (the) block (is) on (the) floor.

2. Variations in word forms that change meaning (two- and three-word phrases)

1. With the child's first efforts to use three-word phrases or sentence combinations, her/his language begins to resemble adult speech. This stage may actually be quite short, assuming a good quality of attention to language, and the child will soon try out an occasional four-word, and even a five-word combination. As noted in the general instructions, grouping words in modular, substitutable two and three word units begins to simplify the problem of holding things in mind (working memory)—also grouping the multiplying relations.

2. The *main task at this phase* is to pick out easy examples of three-word phrases that are made up of

Sequence of Sentence Rules

a. Verb forms (tense and person)

(1) Verb "to be"
Peter is there.
I am here, you are _____, etc.
Carrie was _____, They were
_____, etc. (past tense comes
slowly).
(2) Present progressive, e.g.,
Mary is walking.
Also: I am running, you are going,
etc.
(3) Past-regular verbs, e.g.,
Henry kissed her.
Also: I rocked, you walked, etc.
(4) Past-irregular verbs, e.g.,
Jimmy ate (the) fig.
Harry went outside.
(5) Third person singular, e.g.,
Jane looks (regular verb) out.
Billy does, has (irregular verb) it.
(6) Future tense, e.g.,
Doug will stay.
(will-shall distinction much later)
(7) Imperatives
Run to mama.
Give (me) the book.
(8) Contractions (to be), e.g.,
Mary's here.
I'm in (the) kitchen.
You're on (the) rug.
Also for have, do, can, etc., e.g.,
You haven't (a) cookie.
Charlie hasn't (any) pie.
Don't jump down.
Baby can't walk.

b. Noun forms
(1) Plurals, e.g.,
train-trains (regular)
man-men (irregular)
(2) Possessives, e.g.,
See Harry's toy.

3. Conjunctions
and—(the) bear and (the) lion.
or—(the) boy or girl.
(most other conjunctions, such as if,

Added Points on Stimulation

two, two-word phrases the child has been observed
to use separately. The task is essentially one of combining familiar two-word phrases, such as "a book"
and "big book," into a three-word phrase, "a big
book," or "Polly sit" and "sit down," into "Polly sit
down." Where a child lacks familiarity or ease in using
any specific part of speech in a two-word (pivot type)
combination, special illustrations of such forms should
be provided. This again *illustrates how levels overlap
across age periods.*
This need also points up that, just as two-word combinations are built on initial familiarity with the functions of different parts of speech, so do three-word
phrase combinations build on mastering a wide variety
of different parts of speech in their elementary pivot
term expressions. That is, the child must learn to
manipulate a single set of relations between two terms
(e.g., adjective modifying a noun, "big cat"), together
with the meaning involved, before she/he can be
expected to manage two sets in a three-word combination (e.g., two modifiers of a noun, "a big cat")

| *Sequence of Sentence Rules* | *Added Points on Stimulation* |

Sequence of Sentence Rules

because, but, etc., come later at the next level).

Levels and Starting Ages (Months): III.   18–48+

Four+ Word Sentences

1. Continue to use *basic phrase forms* employed in Level II *according to child's need,* stressing words selectively.

2. Questions

a. Direct questions (beginning with wh—— words, who, whose, what, where, when, why, plus how) to seek specific information , e.g.,
Who wants to jump next?
When do we eat?
What is that?
Where is the bell?
How did you fix it?
b. Yes-no Questions: positive and negative questions with Yes-No answers, e.g.,
Are you going to run? Yes-No
Aren't you going to run?
　Yes (I *am* going to run).
　No (I'm *not* going to run).
The red crayon isn't there, is it?
No (it's *not* there).
Yes (it *is* there).

3. *Joining and rearranging phrase modules and sentences* in complex ways:

a. Agent-action-object combinations, e.g.,
the squirrel runs . . . to the tree
b. *Connecting* terms and phrases *with conjunctions* such as,
(1) *Coordinating relations equally* and:
The white cat *and* the brown rat ran.
The snail slides slowly *and* the snake slides fast.
either-or:
It is a pea *or* a bean.

Added Points on Stimulation

1. *Basic Phrase forms*: At this stage, the child will be familiar with all of the "basic" forms, involving simple agent-action (subject-predicate), noun modifiers (adjectives, articles), verb modifiers (adverbs), prepositional relations, etc.

Most of the attention gradually shifts to using phrases in modular combination (see below), except for *selective attention to any speech forms still presenting difficulty.* Articles, pronouns, and adverbs are among those most likely to need further special attention.
2. Note that the number of words in most of the *single phrases seldom exceeds three or four words,* but in any case much of the need is to *concentrate on the specific terms and relations* with which the child needs help. Thus keep the phrases short, using only the terms necessary (e.g., articles or adjectives, as needed, such as "a cat" versus "the cat").

Once more, where the child continues to encounter difficulty with certain parts of speech or in combining them into two- and three-word phrase relations, specific demonstrations with examples covering the problems should be provided. The principle is always to master the simpler, shorter forms before expecting progress in the more complex, which are made up by putting together the simpler forms in different ways.

3. The scope of the child's mastery of basic phrase forms will be extended by:

a. introducing *more and more examples* of different adjectives, verbs, prepositions, and other forms (increasing vocabulary);
b. *introducing terms for more complex and abstract concepts,* (e.g., delicate, numerical adjectives—two, three, four. . . , colors, width, and depth terms, psychological terms—excited, like, metaphorical uses—covered with gloom, silly air plane. . . , etc.);
c. using long phrases with a string of modifiers, such as "a long, thin, green bean" (adjectives-noun phrase) or "moving slowly and awkwardly" (adverbs-verb phrase).

4. *The task for the various phrase/sentence joining,*

Sequence of Sentence Rules

The spoon is (either) in the drawer *or* on the shelf.

but: It is good *but* cold

(2) *Subordinate (dependency) relations*

because: He can't reach (it), *because* it is (too) high.

if: I can't see *if* you turn out the light.

if-then: *If* the cat jumps, (*then*) he can get across.

unless/until: the ice won't melt *unless* (*until*) it gets warm.

(And gradually many others, e.g., after, before, since, although, etc.).

c. Active-passive voice transformations: (the meaning remains the same but the perspective of acting on or being acted on changes), e.g.,

Nellie pulled the wagon = The wagon was pulled by Nellie.

Sue is painting the picture = The picture is being painted by Sue.

4. Embedding phrases/sentences within sentences:

a. Simple sentences as objects of a sentence

(in agent-action-object relations); *With certain verbs* (with or without "that" (relative pronoun), e.g.,

think—I think (that) *the ball will roll.*

hope—I hope (that) *the dog comes* (when I call).

know—I know (that) *it is hot.*

(others: mean, guess, tall).

b. Indirect Wh—— questions (using where, when, why, whoever, etc.), e.g.,

I know *where* the soap is.

He saw *what* it is.

Does Fran know *when* to start?

Whoever took out the toys should put them away.

c. Relative clauses: whole clauses inserted in a sentence to add information about a key noun (either the subject or an object); may or may not

Added Points on Stimulation

modular rearranging and embedding activities in some ways demands little more in principle than the basic phrase learning activities. The latter is based on combining words to make phrases, or simple two- to three-word phrases to make sentences, e.g.,

a. the + squirrel = the squirrel

b. squirrel + climbs = squirrel climbs

a + b = the squirrel climbs.

The former is simply combining (or arranging) more or less complete phrase and sentence forms, like the following:

a. the red squirrel climbs + the tall tree = the red squirrel climbs the tall tree, or

b. the teacher helped + (when) Muriel fell down = the teacher helped *when* Muriel fell down.

It is evident from the second example (b), however, that there is often a special new term that must be added to join the separate sentences in a meaningful relation (in this case a conjunction to place the first sentence in a dependency relation to the second one). Nonetheless the principle of combining simpler forms and learning how to use the added bridging terms can be taught just as simpler word combining relations are taught: The word "when" needs to be (1) used and illustrated (e.g., by varying the timing of an action) and (2) shown how it works in sentence relations by using different examples of sentence combinations.

Obviously, the number of variations of any form, and the scope and complexity of sentence relations are so great that language development is a process continuing over many years. Infancy and the preschool eras can merely provide a good foundation and an assured interest in language.

5. Note that the sentence play activities with small groups of children (described under general characteristics for sentence rule learning) become especially useful for the complex sentence module joining and rearranging tasks. Children are generally well into the preschool period (past age two or three) before many of these complicated forms can be demonstrated and therefore relatively well advanced in interpersonal play and communication.

Sequence of Sentence Rules   *Added Points on Stimulation*

be introduced by a *relative pronoun,*
i.e., who, whom, which, that), e.g.,
Please give Tom *the toy that you have.*
Sally, *who likes music,* will put on a
record.
The ball *that Grandma gave me*
rolled away.

4

Toy Curriculum

GENERAL CHARACTERISTICS

The toy curriculum provides an outline of major types of common toys and learning materials, organized according to the main concepts and rules they are designed to teach. There are two major types of play materials, structured materials and open-ended materials, each of which take numerous forms. Structured materials lend themselves to manipulation in particular ways that aid a child to learn size, shape, color, object characteristics, and similar specific concepts. Open-ended materials, such as blocks or clay, for the most part offer varied possibilities for constructing or creating novel structures, which in the course of creating the child may experiment with many different concepts.

Not all materials that could be used are included, since such a list would be endless, but representative samples of common and useful types and the various concepts they engender are provided as guidelines for choosing materials and furnishing some idea of what children can learn from different materials. As with the other curricula, the ages indicated are estimates of the ages at which most children can be expected to derive some pleasure and the beginnings of understanding of the concepts involved. The ages are again stated in terms of broad ranges, since differences between children in their readiness to learn or enjoy materials is, as in everything else, enormous. Age is only a very rough index of development. Toys also lend themselves to unexpected uses and interests, which means that infants younger than the lower end of a stated range for a certain toy and children beyond the upper limit may, when given the opportunity, sometimes be found playing with the toy with surprising concentration. Simple curiosity to explore an unfamiliar toy or to explore things that are part of what is known to be the domain of other age groups may be the basis for interest. But children will also make use of form boards, blocks, miniature animals, pictures, and almost anything at all in "nondesign" ways, such as exploring, piling, counting, hiding, placing in containers or incorporating in construction projects or sociodramatic play. While using materials in such varied, "nonfunctional" ways has certain advantages for the imagination, arranging materials in play zones according to age, type and sorts of play is more useful for both concept learning and complex creative development in the long run. Special collections of miscellaneous exploratory, all-purpose materials can always be included in certain zones to supplement or enrich the play.

I. CLOSED STRUCTURE, SPECIFIC PURPOSE MATERIALS

> **Key concepts (cognitive rules) intrinsic to various toy designs***
> **and suggested ages (months) to begin using them.**

A. RIGID STRUCTURES (IMMOVABLE PARTS)

Materials	Concepts and Rules	Age to Begin (Mos.)
Real Objects		
all sizes and shapes; common and uncommon (clothes, household items, tools, community articles)	object constancy object variety: general information of world object characteristics: features and functions, material characteristics such as color, shape, substance, etc. means-ends control: contingency/ causality according to use, problem solving spatial concepts similarity-difference: object types (leads to classification later); discrimination and matching object relations: part-whole; dimensions of size, brightness, weight, etc. sociodramatic-symbolic	2 to 4
Replicas		
miniature copies of objects, common and uncommon (animals, people, vehicles, plants, furniture, clothes, etc.)	same concept series as for real objects representation of things in three dimensional form	6 to 12
occupational and family play materials and props		12 to 18
Pictures and Drawings		
children's books, photos, adult magazines, etc.	representation of things: two dimensionally coded forms, stylized and	6 to 12
diagrams (more abstract)	thus more abstract forms but with greater potential variety, and abstract two dimensional representations	24 to 36

continued

* Certain toys (e.g., clocks, appliances) are often introduced earlier than ages indicated, but simply for object recognition without conceptual elaboration. Nearly all activities involve motor coordination, largely fine motor but a few gross motor tasks are illustrated.

I. CLOSED STRUCTURE (cont.)

Materials	Concepts and Rules	Age to Begin (Mos.)
Miscellaneous Manipulable Small Objects containers (boxes, jars, cans) screens, barriers small hand-sized objects (cubes, sticks, trinkets, gadgets, replicas, etc.) retrieval tools (sticks, rakes, chairs, etc.)	means-ends: problem solving, etc. containment obstacle-detour retrieval search and find	5 to 8
Sensory Materials cotton, sandpaper, sand, wood, metals, clay, etc.	sensory variety: touch, texture, material characteristics: soft-hard, rough-smooth, etc.	12 to 18
Tools and Utensils hammer and hammering board, screwdriver, knife, fork, spoon (used earlier)	means-ends control; variations, contingency/causality, problem solving	18 to 24
Multiple Sets sets of any small, similar (and later dissimilar) materials	object characteristics, variety, and relations spatial concepts means-ends control similarity-differences, leading to classification	30 to 36
Mazes groove (used with stylus), pencil child size (tunnels, wooden and hedge mazes)	means-ends problem solving tracking sequence fine motor skills gross motor skills	24 to 36
Climbing Apparatus walking boards, jungle gym, bars, ladders; climbing logs, forms, etc.	management of body in spatial object structures gross motor modular and hierarchical manipulation principles and coding (balance, coordination, sequence, substitution, subroutines, organization, etc.) alternative means-ends	12 to 18, with equipment scaled to size
Tumbling Mats mats, grass, sand	management of body in relation to gravity, alone or coordinating with others; similar modular and hierarchical coding principles	18 to 30

I. CLOSED STRUCTURE (cont.)

B. MOVABLE STRUCTURES (MOVABLE PARTS)

Materials	Concepts and Rules	Age to Begin (Mos.)
Mobiles		
free moving	movement and gravity	0 to 3
	object constancy, variety, and charac-teristics (as in Section I)	
contingency	means-ends control (as in Section I)	0 to 6
	visual-motor control	
	object characteristics	
Rattles		
rattles, bells, etc.	sound	0 to 3
	movement and gravity	
	means-ends control (as in Section I)	
	visual-motor control	
Live Things	real life object characteristics	
people, animals, plants	life (gradually leading to concepts of growth, development, live systems, and ecological, psychological, and social concepts)	2 to 4, beginning with people
	movement	
Balls		
	roundness	4 to 6
	movement: bouncing, rolling	
	means-ends variations	
Pull Toys		
	means-ends control (as in Section I)	5 to 8
	movement: rolling	
	wheels: roundness, rolling	
	sociodramatic-symbolic	
Devices		
jack-in-the-box, surprise boxes, variable lever doors, variable lock doors	means-ends control: variable alterna-tives	8 to 12
	object constancy	
	surprise	
Mobile Replicas		
simple vehicles	sociodramatic-symbolic	10 to 12
	object constancy, variety, and charac-teristics (see Section I)	
operable and construction vehicles bendable figures	different means-ends activities	18 to 24
	structural-functional relations	

continued

I. CLOSED STRUCTURE (cont.)

Materials	Concepts and Rules	Age to Begin (Mos.)
operable furniture, utensils, and appliances; doll houses	sociodramatic-symbolic: increasing complexity object variety and characteristics (see Section I) classification creative shaping (see Section V)	18 to 24
Sand and Earth dry and wet sand earth (with various tools, containers, replicas)	sociodramatic-symbolic creative-free form (see Section V) means-ends control (as above) characteristics of materials: leads to conservation of substance containment-space	10 to 14
Water Play water and colored liquids (with floating and sinking objects, containers, and sociodramatic replicas)	sociodramatic-symbolic means-ends control (as in Section I) characteristics of materials: states of matter; floating, sinking, density containment-space: leads to conservation of volume	12 to 18, with close supervision
Puppets hand puppets	sociodramatic-symbolic story line (narrative sequence)	18 to 24
Counting and Measuring Sets multi-object sets of discrete small objects (similar and later dissimilar); commercial or home prepared	number concepts: counting, seriation, 1 to 1 correspondence (equivalence), reversibility; addition, subtraction, and other arithmetic operations; conservation of number	18 to 30
multi-object sets varied by length (similar and later dissimilar)	length concepts: measurement, (direct and indirect, i.e., unit measurement) reversibility, arithmetic operations, conservation of length	18 to 30
Mobile Tools pliers, adjustable wrenches, vises, large sewing needles, etc.	means-ends control: variable alternatives	24 to 30
Automatic Devices wind-up toys	independent causality systems variety of means-ends relations	18 to 24

I. CLOSED STRUCTURE (cont.)

Materials	*Concepts and Rules*	*Age to Begin (Mos.)*
watches, clocks, motors, machines, lights, buzzers, etc.	structural-functional relations power, energy, fuel, electricity	24 to 36
Wheel Toys		
walkers, crawlers, kiddy cars, wagons	gross motor skills: mobility in various structural-functional forms; balance, transportation, wheel, etc.	6 to 12
trikes, bikes	complex mobility: balance, transportation, wheel, etc. sociodramatic-symbolic	18 to 30
Swinging, Balancing, Riding Equipment		
swings; rocking and spring horses; rocking boats; see-saws (teeter-totters); circular rides (carousel, swinging rings)	management of body on moving objects (principally balance and postural adjustment to gravity and centrifugal force) alternatives; means-ends control of momentum and balance	8 to 18

C. TAKE APART STRUCTURES (DETACHABLE PARTS)

Materials	*Concepts and Rules*	*Age to Begin (Mos.)*
Put Together Forms		
rings and pegs (ungraded) rods and holed cubes snap beads stringing beads	means-ends control: contingency/causality, problem solving, analysis and synthesis concrete structure: part-whole relations sequence (ungraded)	8 to 12
Puzzles		
jig saw form boards (two dimensional) and shape sorting boxes (three dimensional) (all starting with one to two piece puzzles)	fitting and matching: by shape, size, color, etc. equivalence: 1 to 1 correspondence containment-space object characteristics (see Section I) similarities and differences (see Section I) means-ends relations: problem solving, etc.	10 to 12

continued

I. CLOSED STRUCTURE (cont.)

Materials	Concepts and Rules	Age to Begin (Mos.)
Graded Series		
materials varying in size (length, area, volume): rings and pegs, nesting cups, cubes, and dolls; graded size boards	seriation of quantity, various dimensions	10 to 16
	reversibility	
materials varying in weight	sequence, transitivity	
(use uniformly colored and shaped materials initially)	similarities and differences (see Section I)	18 to 24
Complex Structures		
defined objects built by various connecting mechanisms: bolted or screwed together, having interlocking parts, etc. (vehicles, log cabins, dolls, houses, gas stations, people, etc.)	system organization: hierarchical part-whole relations; analysis-synthesis	24 to 36
	means-ends, problem solving	
	spatial relations: increasingly complex	
	sequence and order	
	object characteristics (see Section I)	
	sociodramatic-symbolic	
Science Kits		
materials for mechanical, electrical, magnifying, chemical experiments, magnets, etc.	means-ends: causality, variable control (see Section I); complex inquiry	24 to 36 according to complexity
	characteristics of materials: processes of different states and types of matter, according to purpose	

II. OPEN STRUCTURE, VARIABLE PRODUCT MATERIALS

A. MODULAR (UNIT) CONSTRUCTION

Materials	Concepts and Rules	Age to Begin (Mos.)
Cubes		
	means-ends	6 to 8
	fine motor skills	
	spatial relations: position, balance, gravity, linear area, verticality, bridging, etc.	
	creative construction (later): modular, variable structure	
Unit Blocks		
table (small) blocks	complex spatial relations: enclosure, curve, level, cantilever, arch, foundation, etc.	12 to 18

II. OPEN STRUCTURE (cont.)

Materials	*Concepts and Rules*	*Age to Begin (Mos.)*
floor blocks (larger—2¼″ × 2¼″ × 1¼″)	creative construction: as above, plus design principles (balance, composition, symmetry, etc.)	16 to 24
large hollow blocks (small)	sociodramatic-symbolic	16 to 24
large hollow blocks (large)	gross motor (macrospheric scale): spatial relations creative construction	24 to 30
Construction Materials with Specialized Mechanisms various shapes and connecting or interlocking mechanisms mechanical construction sets (Meccano or Erector sets, or others with bolt-screw construction) carpentry and various modular craft work projects such as metals or leather (linked to free-form shape cutting)	alternative means-ends connecting mechanisms: dove-tail, gluing, nailing, screwing, snapping, insertion, multiple connections, etc. spatial organizations: cylindrical, oblong, sticklike, angular, etc. two and three dimensional space creative construction design principles: rhythm, symmetry, composition, etc.	30 to 36
Aesthetic Design Blocks various shaped and colored sets of blocks, tiles, mosaics, etc.	design principles: two and three dimensional space	24 to 30

B. FREE FORM (SHAPING)

Materials	*Concepts and Rules*	*Age to Begin (Mos.)*
Two Dimensional finger paints, crayons, drawing materials	creative shaping: creation of forms in space, coding	12 to 18
easel painting, pencil drawing	design principles (shape, color, structure, line, symmetry, etc.)	18 to 24
collage (related to three dimensional and modular materials)	alternative shaping processes: painting —broad flowing control; drawing— refined line control, shading; collage—preshaping (cutting, tearing, selecting)	30 to 36
cutting and shaping engraving control; depth	cutting—removing: combining outlining and drawing engraving—removing: refined line object characteristics; part-whole relations, etc. characteristics of materials	36 to 48

II. OPEN STRUCTURE (cont.)

Materials	Concepts and Rules	Age to Begin (Mos.)
Three Dimensional		
sculpting materials: clay, plasticene, play dough, wax; wet sand or mud using molds	creative shaping: creation of forms in space; coding; design principles (color is less important with three-dimensional materials)	12 to 18
carving materials: soap, soft stone, wood	alternative shaping processes: sculpting, shaping, removing, cutting, shaping characteristics of materials object characteristics, part-whole relations, etc.	36 to 48
Craft Materials		
materials for pounding, denting, bending: metals, leather, wood	alternative creative shaping and organizing processes: shaping through minor alterations in relatively solid materials	24 to 36
weaving, knitting, needlework materials (related to modular crafts)	shaping through interlocking fine-grained linear materials on a two dimensional plane (weaving) design principles as for other media characteristics of materials object characteristics, part-whole relations, etc.	36 to 48

5

Diagnostic-Developmental Monitoring System

For Children Six Months to Six Years Old and their Caregivers

INSTRUCTIONS

So much of the care and education of school age children is organized in terms of groups that many specific aspects of the development of the individual child are often left unattended. Records usually consist of grades for achievements in school learning tasks, but less often embrace processes of socioemotional and cognitive functioning that may affect school achievement and basic development in important ways. On the other hand, when attention is individualized, as is more usual in nursery schools and day care, there is not always a regular record kept of each child's progress in either learning or personality development.

At a time when group care and preschools are becoming more widely established for early development including infancy, it is important that the measures we introduce to assess children's progress do not neglect the processes of how children think and interrelate. A process orientation toward the assessment of each child's styles of development provides insight into how, and thus why, the child does what he or she does, which a record of achievements alone does not provide. This method gives teachers a means of reorienting children toward alternative modes of problem solving and social functioning where their current modes are ineffective or lead to conflict, or of strengthening present styles in those areas where children's ways seem productive and creative.

With some training, assessment of a child can be successfully carried out in the home.

DESCRIPTION OF THE METHODS

This developmental monitoring plan is an instrument for periodically assessing young children's characteristic ways of doing things, in aspects of personality and cognitive processes considered significant for coping and development. Similarly, adults' skills in facilitating such characteristics are assessed using a comparable instrument for caregivers. Processes are classified in eight categories: cognitive style, motivations, object relations, social relations with adults, social relations with peers, representational rules, locomotor skills, and the child's physical state. Each of the six psychological domains encompasses several characteristics, while the child's locomotor skills and physical state are each defined by two. The categories and their characteristics are listed as column headings on the scoring sheets (Diagnostic-Developmental Monitoring Form for Children/Caregivers). Each of the characteristics are defined in the accompanying guide in terms of positive (+) through neutral (0) to negative (−) extremes for the trait in question. When ratings are scored on the more refined seven point scale, the most positive definition is rated as *7* and the most negative definition is rated as *1*. A guide defining the characteristics and the values for ratings at all points along the two different scales that can be used is included.

The scales* have been used extensively in a five year study on day care conducted by the author. The scales were found particularly useful for jointly monitoring the styles of caregivers and the clusters of children for whose development they assumed special responsibility. Each caregiver was asked to look after the week-to-week development of certain children in the group without necessarily tending to all of their daily care. In this way there was always some adult who kept track of all aspects of a child's development, since all children were divided equally among the caregivers. Usually, children were matched with caregivers in terms of how well caregivers felt they got along with the child. Some part of each day would be spent by each caregiver in caring for and observing his or her special charges and talking informally with the other caregivers about how the children were progressing in various ways.

Each cluster of children and their special caregiver were also assessed every two or three weeks (sometimes more frequently) on these diagnostic scales to see how the children were getting along and how well the caregiver was fostering each child's development on the different characteristics. Each child's and caregiver's ratings were compared with previous assessments to give an insight into both the short and long term progress. Reliabilities in the ratings between observers generally ran between .50 and .71, and typically improved with increased use of the scales. The ratings and recommendations for change were discussed each time a child was rated. The entire process proved extremely helpful for staff in working out particular ways for handling the different children's needs. Over the course of several ratings, most caregivers tended to improve in the way they handled their special children and the children correspondingly showed better adaptation in important socioemotional and cognitive processes measured by the scales.

USE OF THE RATING SCALES

These scales are designed to be employed in two major ways: (1) to provide a diagnostic profile of a child's current patterns of functioning; *or* to provide a diagnostic profile of a caregiver's skills in developing optimal functioning for children in his or her charge; and (2) the diagnostic information then serves as a basis for writing a set of recommendations for child care and stimulation and for improving the child-rearing skills of the caregiver. Thus on the same scoring sheet, the teacher, parent, or any caregiver will have available a picture of the child's modes of functioning and a behavioral pres-

* Developed in collaboration with Nasim Khan. See Fowler, W., *Day Care and Its Effects on Early Development: A Study of Group and Home Care in Multi-ethnic, Working Class Families*. Toronto: Ontario Institute for Studies in Education, 1978.

cription of what methods to employ to further the child's or the caregiver's development.

THE RATING SCALES: ASSESSMENT-GUIDANCE FORMS

RATINGS ON CHILD CHARACTERISTICS

The monitoring plan is most easily described through reference to the Assessment-Guidance Form for children, on which the ratings are recorded and recommendations are written. The columns across the top of the page list the child's characteristics or traits of functioning on which he/she is to be rated, each set grouped under the appropriate category. The ratings for each trait are made on the vertical lines extending between the brief positive and negative descriptions of the extremes for the characteristics. More elaborate descriptions of positive (+) and negative (−) extremes are included at the end of this guide. It will again be noted that ratings may be made either in terms of a seven-point scale or by a plus or minus system.

The set of ratings to be made in the vertical rating scales will, when complete, provide a detailed picture of how well a child functions on a variety of significant psychological characteristics.

It will be noted that each of the trait names (analytic, inquisitive, autonomous, etc.) represents a positive end of a psychological dimension. A high rating on autonomy, for example, implies a great deal of self-reliance and ability to assert oneself in the presence of others; a low rating on this dimension implies dependency, passivity, and a general inability to cope on one's own, either alone or in activities with others, without considerable emotional support and/or cognitive guidance. In the same way, a low value on inquisitiveness would imply a dull, monotonous, and unimaginative approach, and a low rating on cooperativeness would imply a highly individualistic or competitive approach.

It is not necessary to rate the child on each characteristic. The activities in which a child is observed may not involve all of the different characteristics. Activities in the physical environment, whether verbal or perceptual-motor, may not, for example, involve social relations; conversely, the usual conversation or sociodramatic play in the verbal medium, if that is the only situation in which the child is observed, would preclude rating the child on object adaptation, though the child could be rated on constructiveness, productivity, and creativity.

The accuracy of ratings will naturally improve with knowledge of the child. Ratings made on a child known intimately, through daily contact in varied situations and milieus over many weeks, can yield more complete, valid, and reliable information than a few observations derived in the course of a day or two in a single setting. It is usually difficult, however, to spend

William Fowler and Nasim Khan

A Guide for Diagnostic Developmental Monitoring (1975)

Child's Name _____ Group _____ Age _____ , for the period _____ to _____ , _____
Date   Date   Adult's Name(s)

Comments

Initial to Final Observation Date:

Fifth to Sixth Observation Date:

Fourth to Fifth Observation Date:

Third to Fourth Observation Date:

Second to Third Observation Date:

First to Second Observation Date:

Cognitive Styles						Motivation				Object Relations				Social Relations										Representation			Motor Skills		Physical State	
														with Adults				with Peers						Verbal		Number	Fine muscle	Large muscle	Energy level	Health
Analytic	Integrative	Reflective	Flexible	Problem oriented	Complex	Inquisitive	Concentrative	Attentive	Persevering	Adaptative	Constructive	Productive	Creative	Cooperative	Adaptive	Autonomous	Empathetic	Cooperative	Adaptive	Autonomous	Empathetic	Comprehension	Production	Pictorial					

Instructions: Each bar is divided into three upper and three lower divisions. Each upper division represents a two point gain (on the 7-point scale) from previous observation. Similarly, each lower division represents a two point loss. The central line in each bar represents no change. Use different colors to show decline as opposed to increase in ratings. Write comments pointing to reasons for changes.

Adult's Progress Assessment Form for Diagnostic Developmental Monitoring (1975)

William Fowler and Nasim Khan

Adult's Name _____ , Group _____ , for the period _____ to _____ ,
Date   Date

Children's Names _____

Children's Ages

Comments

	Cognitive Styles					Motivation					Object Relations				Social Relations								Representation Verbal		Representation	Motor Skills		Physical State	
															with Children				with Peers											
	Analytic	Integrative	Reflective	Flexible	Problem oriented	Complex	Inquisitive	Concentrative	Attentive	Persevering	Adaptative	Constructive	Productive	Creative	Cooperative	Adaptive	Autonomous	Empathetic	Cooperative	Adaptive	Autonomous	Empathetic	Comprehension	Production	Pictorial	Number	Fine muscle	Large muscle	Energy level	Health

Initial to Final Observation Date:

Fifth to Sixth Observation Date:

Fourth to Fifth Observation Date:

Third to Fourth Observation Date:

Second to Third Observation Date:

First to Second Observation Date:

Instructions: Each bar is divided into three upper and three lower divisions. Each upper division represents a two point gain (on the 7-point scale) from previous observation. Similarly, each lower division represents a two point loss. The central line in each bar represents no change. Use different colors to show decline as opposed to increase in ratings. Write comments pointing to reasons for changes.

Reprinted by permission of the authors.

the amount of time necessary to develop a systematic set of ratings. For this reason, ratings can be based on information derived from two sources: (1) firsthand observations by a single rater in as many types of situations as feasible and (2) discussions with other observers, such as day care teachers and supportive staff, and parents, relatives, baby sitters, and others, who through continuous daily or weekly contact may be able to provide more precise information on the child's behavior in other situations.

The amount of time necessary to develop a reasonably accurate set of ratings will of course depend on the clinical and observational skills of the observer. It will also depend on opportunity, the consistency and clarity of a given child's traits, and whether they are expressed in situations available for observation. It is in general more difficult to rate children who are average in many things than those who are high or low on numerous items. Usually, an observer who is unfamiliar with a child should expect to spend several sessions, distributed over two or three days and several distinct areas of activity, to complete an observation series. If a child is already quite familiar to the observer or information is available from informants (parents, teachers, students, etc.), the amount of time needed for observation should decline accordingly. Repeated experience with the use of this observational system, as well as experience with the age group and psychological observation generally, should shorten the time necessary to complete a series to an hour or so.

There is also no reason why the instrument should not be employed selectively. Repeated use with the same child as a method of monitoring critical areas and processes should enable important information to be assembled for communication to teachers weekly or even every other day or so in a few minutes' time on each occasion.

RATINGS ON CAREGIVER CHARACTERISTICS

The Assessment-Guidance Form for Caregivers follows the same pattern as the Children's Form. The observer evaluates the caregiver's behavior that encourages the development of positive characteristics or leads to negative characteristics. The physical, emotional, or verbal interactions of the parent, babysitter, or day care staff may be assessed on a seven-point scale or by a plus or minus system in a manner similar to the children's form.

THE RATING PROFILE

Once the ratings are complete, a line may be drawn between ratings for each characteristic to plot a profile of the child's (or caregiver's) processes, to provide a visual picture of his/her strengths and weaknesses. If ratings are made in terms of the (+), (0) and (−) system, the plots may be placed at the center of the three respective levels (i.e., about opposite the 6, 4, and 2 points of the seven-point scale), thus yielding effectively a three-point scale plot. Where ratings have been omitted connecting lines should probably be omitted. Obviously, the more completely and consistently areas are covered, the more complete and consistent the profile will be.

INTERPRETATIVE SUMMARY BY CATEGORIES

Below the rating profile is a set of spaces for describing in narrative terms the child's manner of functioning or the caregiver's level of fostering such functioning. This method provides an opportunity to paint a qualitative picture, to single out those aspects of functioning that are most salient and explain the dynamics of how and why the child or the caregiver does what he/she does. The section is divided only into the major psychological categories to enable the description to be put together in a more meaningful way, utilizing the available ratings but adding further points about the subject's style that are specific to his/her personality. The space allocated for each category is limited in keeping with the intention of providing periodic, brief analyses of numerous children and caregivers in day care, rather than an extended analysis of each child or caregiver, once or twice a year. Where needed, additional further information can be added on the reverse side of the rating sheet.

GENERAL SUMMARY OF CHILD'S OR CAREGIVER'S STYLES AND PROBLEMS

The final diagnostic section is a completely open space designed for a narrative summary or outline of how the child's or caregiver's ways work together to form his/her personality as a whole. In this description, for the child, the characteristics and how they are manifested from situation to situation would be emphasized. Consistencies, preferred areas of activity, and central problems would be pointed up to attempt to provide an overall understanding of the child's needs and the conditions in her life situation that have made and continue to make her act the way she does, both in positive and negative aspects. Thus conditions, attitudes, and styles in the home would be expected to be central to understanding a child and her history, but patterns in day care might in certain cases contribute to perpetuating both the strong and weak points of a child's personality. There is a strong assumption here that young children, while having the beginnings of definite styles of their own, are relatively open to change through understanding and the application of consistent ways of handling.

In the caregiver's form this summary outlines his strengths and weaknesses in interacting with children, but would not be expected to probe the caregiver's background and life situation with the same detail. It is assumed that awareness and discussion of problem areas would be enough to enable adults to make improvements or build on strengths.

RECOMMENDATIONS FOR CARE
AND STIMULATION

The section at the bottom of the work sheet is intended to serve as a guide for day care staff and teachers (or parents) caring for a child in day to day activities. Using the ratings and interpretive summaries, the rater can write a set of specific methods for working with the child or for improving the skills of the caregiver. The recommendation may be phrased in different ways, for example, one emphasizing immediate, practical techniques to deal with current problems and the other emphasizing long range considerations, which might or might not be feasible to entertain, but which in any case would take time and probably extended effort. Overcrowded home conditions, severe parental illness or death, conflict between parents and grandparents or between day care staff, unsatisfactory job conditions at home or day care, and dysfunctional parental personality styles would fall in the latter category.

A second set might divide into recommendations for teachers and recommendations for parents. These distinctions are useful, depending on the information available from home or day care and the means of implementing alternative approaches in the different settings. Other divisions might be useful, such as recommendations applying to socioemotional as against cognitive processes, or those specific to the several categories or characteristics. None of these are listed, however, to keep the form flexible since each child is likely to need his or her own combination of care methods.

The chief source of information for the recommendations is of course to be drawn from the ratings and interpretations. *The general principle to follow* is to define for teachers (or parents) the kind of experiences specially needed to improve characteristics where the child or caregiver is low (− on the plus or minus rating system or one and two on the seven-point scale). These are problem areas in which extra thought, attention, and perhaps a change in methods of care and stimulation are needed.

For those characteristics and areas in which the subject is average (left blank or marked 0 on the ± system and from three to five on the seven-point system), or above average (+ or six and seven, respectively) less immediate or significant attention is presumably required because these are already areas of relative strength, in which the child is functioning fairly well. These aspects should not be neglected, however, since most individuals can usually learn to cope better in processes in which they function in an average way, given a little guidance, particularly on traits rated on the low side of average (e.g., three on the seven-point scale).

It is also important to take account of the special strengths of the individual (the areas scored + or five to seven), to insure that he continues to encounter conditions that will fortify these strong points to strengthen personality styles along already developing lines. A child who is already highly inquisitive or concentrates well, for example, needs materials, activities, and sufficient order and stimulation in his daily play environment to reinforce these positive trends. An adult who is skilled in arranging play environments for developing complexity needs to be encouraged by being assigned to tasks developing complexity.

It is, however, also true that children can have too much of a good thing. Thus a child high in social adaptiveness, cooperation, and flexibility may be too accommodating and conformist in relating to others, particularly if she is also low in autonomy, perseverance, and reflectiveness, characteristics that are essential for the development of her own cognitive and personal self-system. Recommendations should be considered in the light of how the various traits are *balanced* in some constructive general system of intellectual and emotional coping.

How does one decide upon specific recommendations? Given the principle of providing experiences to help children become, for example, more analytic if they are diffuse or superficial in their approaches to problem solving, the task for adults is to draw attention to the details of objects in learning tasks, encouraging the children to search for relevant detail. The task is usually easier if a child is simply deficient in a single area (fails to perceive particulars or to concentrate when looking at pictures or when listening to statements of peers). A few special sessions with friendly guidance in a setting free from distraction will often do wonders.

Working with a child is more difficult where the child is *generally* undeveloped in some process, such as in reflectiveness, perseverance, or object adaptiveness (interest in things). In these cases the child will need special experience and attentive guidance on the relevant characteristic in many types of situations—with toys, language, pictures, gross motor play, etc. Such children will need help in thinking and reflecting about what they are doing if they are generally low on reflectiveness, that is, impulsive in many different activities. What is needed, in other words, is a *general* change in approach to play and problem solving activities in which the impulsive child is encouraged to take his/her time; helped to play in unpressured play situations (avoiding settings with competitive or quick-acting peers); and in which problems are explored with the child in a slow and thoughtful manner (talking quietly and asking questions about processes—how things work—as opposed to focusing on achievements or outcomes alone). There is, fortunately, usually *some* activity for almost every child in which he/she has some positive interest (object adaptiveness) and is therefore slightly less impulsive. It is often easiest to start guiding the child in new directions with such an area as a point of departure.

Quite often below-level functioning on some aspect of cognitive style or motivation is accompanied by problems in emotional functioning, which show up in specific ways in object relations (destructiveness or low productivity) or social relations (low autonomy—that is, dependency, passivity, and apathy, or poor cooperativeness). In these circumstances the main direction of effort will need to be toward the child's modes of relating to others, particularly toward the significant figures in his/her life situation. Problems of insecurity, elements of rejection by parents, separation anxiety from or emotional dependency on adults are not always even the major source of emotional difficulty. But they are a common source of difficulty that may affect the child's functioning and skill development in many areas. Recommendations for resolving problems like these will lay stress on the socioemotional aspects often implicated in many areas of functioning. Involving both parents and day care staff in discussions of the child's needs for a little extra emotional support and attention, particularly at points of transition between activities, can usually go a long way toward improving a child's self-concept and thus his/her motivation and cognitive styles in many areas. More deep seated or pervasive emotional problems, rooted in family conflicts will, however, usually require professional consultation.

Another source of children's emotional difficulties can be traced to the failure of adults to guide children in knowledge of social rules of cooperation and autonomy, and related rules of object adaptiveness, and constructiveness toward materials, etc. Reared too permissively or restrictively, or neglected, the child may fail to learn and value these attitudes and modes of coping. The child may not be particularly insecure emotionally or hostile toward others, but may simply require definite and consistent redirection in ways of doing things. Concerted and consistent efforts on the part of all day care staff—and preferably coordinated with discussions with the family—will be necessary to develop such modes in children, particularly if the dysfunctional modes have become generalized and habitual.

The particular prescription for each child will thus depend on the nature of the problems and the child's strengths and weaknesses. Whatever they are, recommendations will follow from the particular pattern of functioning with which the child is rated on the assessment form. Wherever socioemotional characteristics show signs of difficulty, special attention will need to be devoted not only to these problems directly but to the manner in which they affect other characteristics of the child's behavior in a number of areas. Keep in mind that the aim of this diagnostic technique is not to make each child function in some theoretically ideal and similar way in every trait and area. Each child will necessarily develop his/her own set of styles of coping and achieving, arising from the particular set of experiences that cumulatively develop his/her own modes of living and striving. The purpose of this monitoring system is merely to resolve some of the difficulties and stimulate the child's strengths in the best manner possible.

Similar prescriptions for a caregiver can be developed on the basis of observed strengths and problems in working with children. An important dimension in the development of caregiving skills in adults is communication

Diagnostic-Development Monitoring Assessment Form for Children (1975)

William Fowler and Nasim Khan

Developmental record of _____, _____, _____ for the period _____ to _____ _____

Child's Name   Group   Age   Date   Date   Name of Adult(s)

Setting (home, day care, indoor, outdoor, free play, guided play, physical care, etc.)

Cognitive Styles						Motivation				Object Relations				Social Relations — With Adults				Social Relations — With Peers				Representation (Verbal)				Loco-motor Skills		Physical State	
Analytic	Integrative	Reflective	Flexible	Problem oriented	Complex	Inquisitive	Concentrative	Attentive	Persevering	Adaptative	Constructive	Productive	Creative	Cooperative	Adaptive	Autonomous	Empathetic	Cooperative	Adaptive	Autonomous	Empathetic	Comprehension	Production	Pictorial	Number	Fine motor	Gross motor	Energy level	Health

Top scale (top of each column):

| Focuses on significant details | Puts things together | Thinks before acting | Adaptive | Perceptive of problems | Likes complex things | Explores the unfamiliar | Highly absorbed | Follows an activity | Overcomes obstacles | Likes things | Uses material positively | Accomplishes things | Original combinations | Interacts constructively | Friendly and trustful | Shows initiative | Sensitive to others' needs | Interacts constructively | Friendly and trustful | Shows initiative | Sensitive to others' needs | Excellent understanding of language | Excellent speech/ babbling | Excellent use of pictures | Excellent understanding of numbers | Excellent use of fine muscles | Excellent use of large muscles | Functions at a high level of energy | Maintains excellent health |

Scale: 7, +6, 5, 0 4, 3, −2, 1

Bottom scale (bottom of each column):

| Overlooks significant details | Disorganized | Impulsive | Rigid | Poor awareness of problems | Likes simple things only | No interest in the unfamiliar | Loses interest easily | Scattered attention | Gives up easily | Little interest in things | Destructive | Finishes no product | Unimaginative combinations | Very little constructive interaction | Withdrawn | Aggressive | Passive dependent | Attention demanding | No awareness of others' needs | Very little constructive interaction | Withdrawn | Aggressive | Passive dependent | Attention demanding | No awareness of others' needs | Little understanding of language | Little speech/ babbling | Little use of pictures | Little understanding of numbers | Poor use of fine muscles | Poor use of large muscles | Functions at a low level of energy | Maintains poor health |

	Cognitive Styles	Motivation	Object Relations	Social Relations — With Adults	Social Relations — With Peers	Representation	Motor Skills	Physical State
Comments on child's patterns in different areas								
Summary of adult's strengths and problems								
Suggested methods for improving child's development and learning								

Reprinted by permission of the authors.

Diagnostic-Developmental Monitoring Assessment Form for Caregivers (1975)

William Fowler and Nasim Khan

Profile of _____ , _____ for the period _____ to _____ _____
           Caregiver's Name   Group   Date   Date   Child(ren)'s Name(s)

Setting (home, day care, indoor, outdoor, free play, guided play, physical care, etc.)   Age(s)

Cognitive Styles	Motivation	Object Relations	Social Relations — With Adults	Social Relations — With Peers	Representation	Loco-motor Skills	Physical State

Encourages Child to:

Column headings (top labels / "Encourages Child to:"):

Cognitive Styles: Analytic (Focus on significant details); Integrative (Put things together); Reflective (Think before acting); Flexible (Adapt); Problem oriented (Perceive problems); Complex (Like complex things)

Motivation: Inquisitive (Explore the unfamiliar); Concentrative (Be highly absorbed); Attentive (Follow an activity); Persevering (Overcome obstacles)

Object Relations: Adaptive (Like things); Constructive (Use material positively); Productive (Accomplish many things); Creative (Original combinations)

Social Relations — With Adults: Cooperative (Interact constructively); Adaptive (Be friendly and trustful); Autonomous (Develop initiative); Empathetic (Be sensitive to others' needs)

Social Relations — With Peers: Cooperative (Interact constructively); Adaptive (Be friendly and trustful); Autonomous (Develop initiative); Empathetic (Be sensitive to others' needs)

Representation (Verbal): Comprehension (Excellent understanding of language); Production (Excellent speech/babbling); Pictorial (Excellent use of pictures); Number (Excellent understanding of numbers)

Loco-motor Skills: Fine motor (Excellent use of fine muscles); Gross motor (Excellent use of large muscles)

Physical State: Energy level (Function at a high level of energy); Health (Maintain excellent health)

Scale: 7, +6, 5, 4, 3, −2, 1 (left side) and 7, 6+, 5, 4, 3, 2−, 1 (right side)

Leads Child to: (bottom labels)

Cognitive Styles: Overlook significant details; Be disorganized; Impulsiveness; Rigidity; Poor awareness of problems; Like simple things only

Motivation: Lack of interest in the unfamiliar; Lose interest easily; Scattered attention; Giving up easily

Object Relations: Little interest in things; Destructiveness; Finishing no product; Unimaginative combinations

Social Relations — With Adults: Very little constructive interaction; Withdrawing; Aggression; Passive dependence; Attention demanding; No awareness of others' needs

Social Relations — With Peers: Very little constructive interaction; Withdrawing; Aggression; Passive dependence; Attention demanding; No awareness of others' needs

Representation: Little understanding of language; Little speech/babbling; Little use of pictures; Little understanding of numbers

Motor Skills: Poor use of fine muscles; Poor use of large muscles

Physical State: Function at a low level of energy; Maintain poor health

Cognitive Styles	Motivation	Object Relations	Social Relations — With Adults	Social Relations — With Peers	Representation	Motor Skills	Physical State
Comments on patterns in different areas							
Summary of strengths and problems							
Suggested methods for improving caregiving skills							

Reprinted by permission of the authors.

of the weaknesses. Written statements need to be supplemented with personal discussion. If possible, make self-evaluations via videotape or film in conjunction with the observer's discussions.

PROGRESS ASSESSMENT FORMS

Summary graphs showing changes from initial to later observations are made on the Children's Progress Assessment Form or the Caregiver's Progress Assessment Form. Each vertical bar is divided in the middle by a wide horizontal line. The three narrower horizontal lines on the upper portion are used for marking increases in ratings compared to the previous rating. The lower portion of the vertical bar is used to show declines. A rise or decline of two points on the seven-point rating scale is represented by one interval between two of the narrow horizontal lines on the progress assessment form. Each interval also represents one value (+, 0, or −) on the three-point plus-or-minus system of scoring. It can be helpful to use different colors to designate rises and declines.

Another way of evaluating changes is to use transparencies of individual diagnostic monitoring forms to study the overlay of two observations.

Scoring System for
Diagnostic-Developmental Monitoring

PLUS-MINUS RATING SYSTEM

+   above average, highly characteristic

−   below average, not at all characteristic

0   within an average range

?   uncertain or insufficient information

/   does not appear applicable

SEVEN-POINT SCALE RATING SYSTEM

Plus statement (+)

7—highly characteristic or salient

6—quite characteristic or salient

5—somewhat characteristic or salient

Middle Level (0)

4—neither upper statement nor lower statement is characteristic or salient— or both apply equally (at different times)

Minus statement (−)

   3—somewhat characteristic or salient

   2—quite characteristic or salient

   1—highly characteristic or salient

Score items on the basis of the average developmental levels culturally expected for his or her age.

Note: Both childrens' and adults' assessment forms follow the above scoring system. However, the ratings of adults' behavior evaluate the extent to which they encourage or discourage children in comparable characteristics described below.

DEFINITIONS OF CATEGORIES AND CHARACTERISTICS

COGNITIVE STYLES

(Modes of looking, manipulating, and thinking in the course of solving problems, and constructing or creating things and/or interrelating with others).

Analytic

+   child focuses on details, features of objects, objects in a field, isolated relations.
−   child attends to no single feature or object, has global approach to objects or situations, overlooks even important features, objects, and relationships.

Integrative

+   child concentrates on putting things together; looks for patterns and organizations; has synthetic approach, tends to organize things.
−   child has diffuse, scattered approach, disorganized, does not connect things.

Reflective

+   child deliberates before responding, tends to work out a problem mentally.
−   child tends to act without thinking, comes to decisions prematurely, very quickly; impulsive.

Flexible

+   adaptive to changing circumstances; tries out different approaches when one does not work.
−   rigid, gets upset over changing circumstances, fails to adapt or try different ways.

Problem Oriented

+   perceptive of problems and conflicts; oriented toward searching for and reaching solutions; enjoys working on problems.
−   little awareness of problems; glosses over or avoids problems; little interest in working at or solving problems.

Complexity

+   seeks complex or difficult activities, tasks and forms of play; enjoys challenge.

— prefers simple things; generally chooses materials and activities easy for his or her developmental level.

MOTIVATION

(Strength and type of desire to achieve, solve problems, and construct things
and interrelate with others).

Inquisitiveness

+   actively explores and examines environment, concerned with how things work and curious about differences, discrepancies, and the novel; points inquiringly to objects, asks questions if he/she is able.

—   disinterested, plays in dull repetitive fashion largely with familiar toys and routines; unexcited by change or the unfamiliar.

Concentration

+   centers attention on objects or tasks for long periods and is not easily distracted; becomes highly absorbed in task.

—   easily loses interest; fleeting attention, constant shifting of attention from one activity to another.

Attentiveness

+   watches and follows a demonstration of a toy, picture or activity with alertness; responds readily to attempts to get his/her attention.

—   difficult to capture and maintain attention; resists efforts to interest him/her in an activity or demonstration.

Perseverance

+   perseveres in the face of obstacles; tries hard to overcome obstacles, works until the task is completed well.

—   gives up easily in the face of obstacles; purposeless random activity.

OBJECT RELATIONS

(Orientation toward and modes of interrelating with things, including plants
and animals, but excluding people).

Object Adaptation

+   child is positively oriented toward play with toys and activity with things generally; has definitely developed interests, but adapts reasonably to change and novel objects, whether or not he/she is curious about change, novelty, or how things work.

—   child is timid, fearful, has little sustained interest in activities with toys or other materials; adapts poorly or is indifferent to change.

Constructiveness in Play

+ makes positive use of materials; sensitive to the nature of materials, cares that objects, plants, animals, etc., are used to good purpose.

− aggressively destructive in use of materials; frequently breaks or ruins materials.

Productive

+ produces large number of finished products or a highly differentiated single product.

− produces no products.

Creative

+ combines things in unusual, original, imaginative ways or creates new elements, not stereotyped.

− constantly reproduces highly familiar elements, makes only stereotyped combinations.

SOCIAL RELATIONS

(Orientations toward and modes of interrelating with adults or peers)

Cooperative

+ actively seeks to work out problems in cooperation with others, is sensitive to needs and requests of others, shares, takes turns.

− is unable to work in cooperation with others; shows no initiative in proposing solutions; may often be found working alone; may be highly individualistic or competitive.

Socially Adaptive

+ child approaches another person with friendliness and trust; participates in group activities but also enjoys play alone.

− child is aloof and withdrawn, is not happy among people or is persistently and strongly aggressive in work or play, often without provocation.

Autonomous

+ independent, shows initiative and self-reliance in coping, alone or with others; can cope with unexpected frustrations.

− child either shows no initiative and is generally passive, pliable, or dependent on others; or constantly seeks attention of and clings to others.

Empathic (Empathetic)

+ aware of, sensitive to, and identifies with psychological needs and states of others.

− shows little or no awareness of, sensitivity to, or identification with psychological needs and states of others.

REPRESENTATIONAL RULES

Verbal Comprehension

+ child has excellent comprehension of spoken language.

− child has very little understanding of language.

Verbal Production

\+   child babbles a lot or verbalizes at a very high level, depending on age.

\—   child shows very little babbling or speech.

Pictorial

\+   shows great interest in pictures and their details.

\—   shows very little interest in pictures or picture books.

Number

\+   shows high interest in numbers, enjoys counting and measuring (length, width, area); interested in numerals.

\—   shows very little interest in number activities; counting (either rote or one-to-one correspondence), measuring, or in numerals.

LOCOMOTOR

Fine motor

\+   excellent skills in fine motor activities, such as manipulating tiny objects, placing pegs in holes, cutting with scissors, stringing beads.

\—   poor skills in fine motor activities.

Gross motor

\+   excellent skill in large muscle activities, such as running, climbing, bicycle riding, ball throwing.

\—   very little skill in large muscle activities.

PHYSICAL STATE

Energy Level

\+   highly active, continues in activities for a long time without apparent fatigue. (Real energy, not nervous energy, not hyperactivity.)

\—   highly passive, tires easily, lies around, requires an excessive amount of sleep.

Health

\+   subject to very few illnesses such as colds; recovers quickly from illness; no specific continuing infection (such as eczema or chronic nasal drip).

\—   chronically ill with several specific health problems, easily catches infections, recovery often prolonged.

6

Environmental Profile

A Method for Assessing the Educational and Socioemotional Quality of Day Care Environments

NATURE AND PURPOSE OF THE
ENVIRONMENTAL PROFILE

With the current rapid spread of day care and school centers for infants and preschool children throughout the world there is a definite need to ensure that quality is not sacrificed in the face of accelerating demands for group care, however great and legitimate the need. Certainly we may anticipate an expanding demand for such facilities, given the growing economic and psychological needs of women to seek jobs and careers outside the home.

The very urgency of the demand and the lack of historical preparation in the development of programs, methods, standards, and training of staff for infant and child day care creates a critical social problem not easily met. For one thing, socialization of children in the early years has been predominantly carried out by women in the home whose efforts have not been calculated economically on the labor market. It is therefore probable that society, where men occupy most of the critical positions of social decision making, is ill-prepared to face the costs of staffing these new day care centers on a realistic basis. This is despite the fact that theoretically we are not adding new costs but merely calculating the real value of women's contributions to society for the first time. The shock is difficult to absorb.

The establishment of day care and nursery school centers throughout Canada and the United States has coincided with a rising body of information illustrating the critical importance of early experience to the development of children. Some children may even benefit from newly established centers of a poor standard, because the limited quality of care may still be an improvement upon their own home conditions. But the substitution of a lesser evil can hardly be justified as a legitimate solution to society's and children's needs for proper care in the early years. Moreover, most families of *all* classes and regions in society are accustomed to ensuring that their children receive adequate care in the early years, and they will not be prepared to sacrifice this care in the interests of a short-sighted economy that will stunt the development of a whole generation of children. But more than this, our knowledge of what constitutes good care and education in the early years has progressed far beyond the average levels culturally provided in many homes. The pooling of resources in group day care settings makes possible a level and variety of individually oriented child care much beyond the practices of the past.

The development of standards and quality methods will, of course, come about through the development and application of knowledge about children, child rearing, and child development. The establishment of programs with well-defined objectives and tested methods based on knowledge and humanistic values will do much to bring about the development of quality care for young children. There is also need, however, to assess how well objectives and methods are realized in practice. Too often there is a large gap between intentions and experience, between competence and performance. Institutional economics and politics often force compromises even where competence is amply available and, since the field is so new, knowledge and competence are still poorly developed and in short supply.

For these reasons, an instrument that is comprehensive and well defined, relatively easy to administer, and details a method of assessing the adequacy of group care facilities and programs may contribute much toward the development, extension, and realization of standards. To this end we have designed a set of scales intended to define *performance standards* and *operating conditions* essential to the functioning of quality group care for young children.

The scales* have been used for research and other purposes to assess program quality in a wide variety of early childhood day care centers and school settings, including municipally, privately, and university operated programs, and parent cooperatives. In the author's longitudinal investigation on day care, reported in the book entitled *Day Care and Its Effects on Early Development: A Study of Group and Home Care in Multi-ethnic Working Class Families,* Toronto: Ontario Institute for Studies in Education, 1978, the scales were used to pinpoint strengths and weaknesses in the program as implemented over two program years. On the total five sets of scales, the reliability of ratings between observers ranged between .51 and .86 ($\bar{x}$ = .70), (excluding one deviant rating). In another study designed to evaluate the quality of eleven day care centers operated by a single municipality, it was found that the reliability between two independent observers for ratings in the two scales measured (Form 2, Adult Social Structure and Socioemotional Environment, and Form 3, Structuring of Children's Socioemotional Environment), reached .98. Correlations between their mean ratings and the cost of operating the centers, moreover, was .61, pointing up the difficulty of providing quality care on low budgets. As a result of this experience in these and other studies, the scales have been revised for this book.

The scales are intended to be administered by any person, regardless of role or the type of day care or preschool institution to which he/she is attached, who is attempting to define and develop standards for early group care. Among those likely to find the scales useful are persons in public and private agencies, including business organizations and unions, responsible for the administration and development of day care institutions, programs, and standards in the community; professional nursery school and day care staff, teaching organizations, and centers attempting to develop day care programs; and parents, teachers, and parent-teacher cooperatives attempting to define and develop adequate day care and preschool programs for their children.

---

* Developed in collaboration with Karen Ogston.

DESIGN OF THE SCALES

The scales are intended for use with children in programs from birth up to school age (about five to six years). Except for teacher-child ratios, most of the dimensions of the scales are not defined in terms of age, but can be readily applied to evaluating programs for any of the preschool age ranges. Although no particular type of program is defined, the scale descriptions are designed according to principles and methods for producing more humanistic interpersonal relations between adults and children, and for encouraging desirable forms of socioemotional, perceptual-motor, language, and cognitive development in children. Many types of spatial arrangements, toys, and equipment can fulfill the definitions of a quality program, varying from crude homemade models to beautifully tooled, high cost hardwood educational materials. There are, on the other hand, certain characteristics and *principles in the design of certain toys* that best stimulate interest, the desire to explore, and creative construction and problem solving activities in children. By the same token, although many human beings can enjoy and contribute much to young children's development, certain personality styles and approaches tend to enrich and develop children's feelings and understanding more than others.

The scales are designed with the assumption that all categories of experience—physical, social, and intellectual—are major sources of development and learning. To this end the set of scales covers a number of dimensions organized into five major areas, as follows:

Form 1:   Physical environment
Form 2:   Adult social structure and socioemotional environment
Form 3:   Structure of children's socioemotional environment
Form 4:   Cognitive stimulation program
Form 5:   Toys and equipment

SCORING SYSTEM

The scales themselves consist of two sections, a *Profile Sheet* and a longer section, the *Scale Descriptions,* containing a detailed description of the characteristics or scale dimensions on which the center and its program is to be assessed. Ratings should be marked at the appropriate points along the scales on the profile sheets only after studying carefully the relevant textual description. It is assumed that the rater is either already currently familiar with the school, center or age or play group within a center to be rated or has the opportunity and takes the time to observe the center in operation and discuss the program with staff and parents before rating, a process which may require from a few hours to a few days, depending on the experience of the rater both in early child care and with the scales themselves. In the course of scoring items, frequent reference to the dimensional descriptions may be useful, particularly during the first use of the scales.

Each of the subordinate categories listed in the outline above embraces a number of dimensions defined in terms of seven-point scales, ranging from a low value of one to a high value of seven. Every dimension has three basic levels, the extremes of low and high, or one and seven on the scales, and the center level of the scale midpoint of four. The lowest level, one, represents poor, well below minimum standards for the dimension in question, point 4 represents moderate performance or adequate quality, while the top level, seven, represents very high quality. It is assumed that many centers or playroom groups within a center are likely to score slightly below or slightly above the value of 4 on many dimensions, so that values from 3 to 5 inclusive would be a normally expected operating range. A value of 2 would represent a clear deficit for a specific dimension, though not as grossly deficient as the lowest value of 1. Anything above 5 on the scale, on the other hand, from 6 to 7, would be definitely *above* average, probably found only in a few laboratory research oriented schools and centers.

The scale values and their meanings may be summarized as follows:

Scale Values	Standards	Profile Sheet
1 2 3 }	Deficient	Low
4 5 }	Acceptable Range	Adequate
6 7 }	High Level–Exceptional	Excellent

A number of the dimensions have two numerical scale systems attached, as, for example, where teacher-child ratios, number of toys, or percentage figures to indicate the proportion of staff sharing certain teaching characteristics require a separate numerical scaling system. The second scaling system has been assigned values along with the same one- to seven-point scale *in parallel,* however, so that values on any of the dimensions can be compared quantitatively.

In the *Scale Descriptions,* each of the three basic levels (1, 4, and 7) of many of the separate dimensions are described to clarify the meaning of each level for every dimension. Values between the three major levels can be interpolated with reference to the descriptions assigned to the basic levels.

In addition to providing general profiles for each of five categories and an estimate of performance quality for every characteristic, ratings can be averaged to provide information on how a center performs generally in each category and subcategory. By taking the mean ratings for all dimensions in the Cognitive Stimulation Program (Form 4), for example, we can obtain a good, general picture of the quality of education for a given school or center. At the most general level, the rating values for the entire set of dimensions for the total set of scales may be averaged to indicate the overall quality of a center. On a more selective basis, it may be useful to average ratings on the separate item clusters within a total profile category or form to provide information, for example, on how a center fosters creative and construction activity in children.

Environmental Profile

Form 1: Physical Environment

Name of Center: _____
Address: _____
Phone: _____
Observer: _____
Date(s) of Observation: _____

		Multi-purpose Space (check)*	1	2 Low	3	4 Adequate	5	6 Excellent	7
Indoor Space		Total Quantity	≤35	40	45	50	55	60	≥70
	Distribution: Child Areas (sq. ft. per child)	General play	≤25	30	35	40	45	50	≥55
		Gross motor play	none	30	35	40	45	50	≥55
		Eating areas	none	10	11	12	13	14	≥15
		Sleeping areas	none	20	21	22	23	24	≥25
		Extra purpose rooms (No. per center)	none	1	2	3	4	5	≥6
		Dressing-change areas	≤2	3	4	5	6	7	≥8
		Other space	none	1	2	3	4	5	≥6
	Bathroom Facilities	Toilets (child-size) – unit-child ratio	≤1:9	1:8	1:7	1:6	1:5	1:4	≥1:3
		Washbasins (child-size) – unit-child ratio	≤1:9	1:8	1:7	1:6	1:5	1:4	≥1:3
	Staff-parent Facilities	Lounge-coffee room (sq. ft. per adult)	≤25	28	31	34	37	40	≥43
		Office space (desk-adult ratio)	≤1:5	1:4	1:3	1:2	2:3	3:4	≥1:1
Outdoor Space		Total Quantity	≤30	40	50	60	70	80	≥90
	Distribution: Child Areas (sq. ft./child)	Soft surface	≤15	20	25	30	35	40	≥45
		Hard surface	≤15	20	25	30	35	40	≥45
		Nature Garden	0	5	10	15	20	25	≥30

Notes (Comment also on particular strengths or weaknesses including any not covered by the scale.)

*Multi-purpose space: place a check in top row over each item in which facility is used for more than one group or activity on a rotating basis.

153

Form 1

Physical Environment

SPACE-INDOOR

QUANTITY—ALL ACTIVITIES

Square feet per child (excluding radiators, cabinets, toy shelves, change tables, cribs, adult furniture, etc., but including child-sized furniture)

range: $\leq 35-\geq 70$ square feet per child

DISTRIBUTION: CHILD AREAS

General play (excluding gross motor play)   Square feet per child as above, (excluding radiators, cabinets, etc.)

range: $\leq 25-\geq 55$ square feet per child

Gross motor play   Square feet per child (exclusive of all furniture except gross motor apparatus itself, i.e., climbing apparatus, tunnels, walking boards, vehicles, pull toys, tumbling mats, large hollow blocks, etc.)

range: none$-\geq 55$ square feet per child

Eating areas   Square feet per child (exclusive of all equipment except children's tables and chairs).

range: none$-\geq 15$ square feet per child

Sleeping rooms (separated)   Square feet per child (exclusive of everything except cribs, cots, etc.)

range: none$-\geq 25$ square feet per child

Extra purpose rooms   Number of rooms at least $5' \times 7'$ each suitable for small group free or guided play, for special activities, segregated play, or use as quiet area for contagious children, parent or visitor discussions, testing, etc.

range: none$-\geq 6$ rooms per center

Dressing-change areas   Square feet per child (excluding children's lockers, toilets, change tables, protruding cabinets, furniture, etc.)

range: $\leq 2-\geq 8$

Other space   Space, such as hallways, vestibules, etc., not designed for a particular child use, but which can provide extra child areas.

range: none–≤ 6 square feet per child

BATHROOM FACILITIES

1. *Number of appropriate size toilets*   (For toilet trained children or children in training. Small size for children under four years of age. Adult size for children over four years of age.)

range: ≤ 1:9–≥ 1:3 units per child

2. *Number of child-sized washbasins*   Small size for children under four years of age. Adult size for children over four years of age.

range: ≤ 1:9–≥ 1:3 units per child

STAFF-PARENT FACILITIES

1. *Lounge-coffee room*   Square feet per adult including furniture.

range: ≤ 25–≥ 43

2. *Office space*   Desk-adult ratio (staff or cooperating parents, exclusive of director or supervisor).

range: ≤ 1:5–≥ 1:1 units per adult

SPACE-OUTDOOR

QUANTITY—ALL PLAY ACTIVITIES

Square feet per child including equipment but exclusive of storage and nature areas.

range: ≤ 30–≥ 90 square feet per child

DISTRIBUTION: CHILD AREAS

Soft surface   Square feet per child of lawn, soft ground, tan bark, or similar resilient material for movement play, climbing apparatus, teeter totters, swings, horses, sociodramatic structures such as houses, boats, etc.

range: ≤ 30–≥ 90 square feet per child

Hard surface   Square feet per child of asphalt, concrete, hard ground, etc. for rideable wheel toys, hollow blocks, sand boxes, etc.

range: ≤ 15–≥ 45 square feet per child

Nature garden area   Square feet per child of trees, shrubs, flowers, special garden and digging areas, etc.

range: ≤ 10–≥ 40 square feet per child

Environmental Profile

Form 2: Adult Social Structure and Socioemotional Environment

Name of Center: _____
Address: _____
Phone: _____
Observer: _____
Date(s) of Observation: _____

		1 Low 2 3 4 Adequate 5 6 Excellent 7	
Administration	Leadership makes all decisions		Staff cooperates in decision making
Staff Cooperation	No coordination of planning efforts		Highly cooperative planning
Psychological Atmosphere	Closed—restrained		Open—expressive
Schedules	Rigid		Flexible
Parent Involvement	Excluded from decisions		Highly involved in decisions
Community Relations	Superficial contact with community resources		Regular planned relations with community resources
Staff Qualification	Director only is trained in child care		All staff highly trained (formerly or informally)
In-service Education	No staff development program		Productive staff development program
Staff Evaluation	No systematic evaluation		All staff involved in systematic evaluation

Notes

(Comment also on particular strengths or weaknesses including any not covered by the scale.)

Form 2

Adult Social Structure and Socioemotional Environment

GROUP ORGANIZATION AND ADULT RELATIONS WITHIN THE CENTER, AND BETWEEN THE CENTER AND HOME AND COMMUNITY

ADMINISTRATION: DECISION MAKING PARTICIPATION OF CENTER PERSONNEL

LOW: Decision making restricted entirely to leadership (director, board, head teachers, etc.). Limited communication to staff (often for reasons of policy), and limited opportunity for discussion of problems and decisions.

ADEQUATE: Most staff members participate in decisions. Formal or informal meetings are regularly held.

EXCELLENT: All staff members participate through explicit decision-making procedures, such as open meetings, voting, rule formulation, etc. Regular discussions are held to analyze problems in routines, attitudes, and methods of cooperation.

STAFF COOPERATION

LOW: No planning or coordination of individual efforts or interactions.

ADEQUATE: Regular cooperation among most staff members.

EXCELLENT: All professional and nonprofessional staff members cooperate frequently; many tasks are planned and implemented jointly by two or more persons.

OPENNESS OF PSYCHOLOGICAL ATMOSPHERE

LOW: Noticeable absence of warmth, natural expression of feeling, and spontaneous verbalization.

ADEQUATE: Moderate informality, friendliness, expressivity, spontaneous verbalization and openness of interaction.

EXCELLENT: Noticeably friendly, warm, expressive, and personalized atmosphere.

SCHEDULES AND RULES

LOW: A preoccupation with rules and rigid schedules that put restrictive limits on almost all activities.

ADEQUATE: Rules and schedules create few problems and do not noticeably conflict with ongoing activity patterns.

EXCELLENT: Well-planned system of flexible scheduling in terms of approximate blocks of time, types of activity, and teacher and child roles and responsibilities, rather than fixed times, tasks, and rules. Rules and schedules allow relaxed, smooth, and comfortable transitions between activities.

PARENT INVOLVEMENT AND RELATIONS

LOW: Parents have no voice in policy, decision making, or program planning.

ADEQUATE: Some participation by parents through periodic meetings, reports on children, and similar arrangements.

EXCELLENT: Parents contribute strongly to policy decision making and regularly participate in group discussions of organization and program planning. Parents are represented on a board and on working committees concerned with policy making and program development. Parents exercise control as parents. Extensive teacher-parent conferences.

COMMUNITY RELATIONS: RELATIONS BETWEEN CENTER AND LOCAL COMMUNITY AND OTHER INSTITUTIONS

LOW: Little more than superficial formal or business contact.

ADEQUATE: Numerous relations with other organizations and some relations with individuals in the local community.

EXCELLENT: Regular relations, both formal and informal, with other organizations (neighborhood, social, cultural, business, etc.) for the purpose of mutual self-help and promotion of children's community relations and social development. Regular relations with individuals, families, and facilities in the neighborhood through visits and excursions. Staff participate in community projects.

STAFF QUALIFICATIONS

LOW: Hardly any staff, including the administrator of the center, has any education or supervised professional experience as a day care worker or nursery school or preschool teacher.

ADEQUATE: The administrator and some staff are trained in child development and early education and have some professional experience as day care workers or preschool teachers. In a parent-cooperative center, an organized in-service education program exists.

EXCELLENT: The center is supervised by a well-trained teacher or day care worker with a staff highly trained in early education and child development and thoroughly experienced in professionally run settings in day care or other preschools. In the case of a parent cooperative, all staff are highly competent and involved in a strong in-service education program utilizing professional resources.

INSERVICE EDUCATION: STAFF DEVELOPMENT

LOW: Little or no effort to stimulate staff understanding of and interest in child development or adult social relations.

ADEQUATE: A regular in-service development program including assigned staff reading, discussion, and demonstration of techniques with involvement of skilled resource persons.

EXCELLENT: Regular and frequent reading, discussion, and demonstration of techniques for enhancing child development and both child and adult interpersonal relations. This includes continuing evaluation and case studies of individual children, associated with close involvement of highly skilled staff with other resource persons.

STAFF COMPETENCE EVALUATION

LOW: No systematic methods for hiring, promotion, or dismissal. Rely on intuitive, undefined statements by a director or leadership group.

ADEQUATE: Periodic evaluation and involvement of staff in their own evaluations, some objective measures used.

EXCELLENT: All staff regularly involved with leadership through discussion and observation in systematic analysis of their own and other members' methods and styles using both informal and objective ratings. A close relationship exists between evaluation and in-service education programming.

Environmental Profile

Form 3: Structure of Children's Socioemotional Environment

Name of Center: _____
Address: _____
Phone: _____
Observer: _____
Date(s) of Observation: _____

			1	2 Low	3	4 Adequate	5	6 Excellent	7	
Staff-Child Ratios	Pre- and semi-mobile infants		1:>6	1:5	1:4	1:3	1:2	1:1	1:<1	12 months
	Beginning autonomy		1:>7	1:6	1:5	1:4	1:3	1:2	1:<2	13 – 24 months
	Relative autonomy		1:>8	1:7	1:6	1:5	1:4	1:3	1:<3	25 – 36 months
	High autonomy		1:>9	1:8	1:7	1:6	1:5	1:4	1:<4	37 – 48 months
	Group development		1:>10	1:9	1:8	1:7	1:6	1:5	1:<5	49 – 60 months
Organizational Characteristics	Continuity	No provision for continuity								One caregiver several times a day for 6 months
	Multiple relations	Limited exposure in few roles								Regular exposure in varied roles
	Flexibility and structure	Highly over or under organized schedules and relations								Balance between flexibility and structure in all aspects of program
Caregiving – Teaching Styles	Warmth	Cold, impersonal								Warm and positive
	Perceptiveness	Unperceptive								Perceptive
	Adaptiveness	No variation in style								Style varied with circumstances
	Autonomy	No balance between autonomy and dependency								Balance between autonomy and dependency
	Cooperation	No encouragement of cooperative work or play: authority-child centered								Cooperative situations devised for work and play: child-child centered
Program Social Goals	Cultural diversity	Culturally homogeneous								Regular exposure to representative diversity
	Play and work	Little attention to work/play balance								Careful programming of work and play development
	Encouragement of friendship	No encouragement								Relations regularly appraised to foster constructive friendship
	Sociodrama and diversification of sex roles	Stereotyped and unvaried sex and work roles in play								Sociodramatic diversity in themes and work roles for both sexes
	Evaluation of socioemotional development	No systematic observations								Regular systematic observations

Notes (Comment also on particular strengths or weaknesses including any not covered by the scale.)

Form 3

Structure of Children's Socioemotional Environment

AVERAGE DAILY ON FLOOR STAFF-CHILD RATIOS

(teachers, assistants, parents, students in training, volunteers, older children) who are at hand for child care but not necessarily tending to children. *Note:* Consider only number of staff when full complement of children for any part of the day are present (i.e., 9 A.M.–5 P.M.). Ratios may change during the course of the day, which should be reflected in the ratio reported.

PRE- AND SEMI-MOBILE INFANTS

($\leq$ 12 months: highly dependent, little or no language comprehension and speech; limited instrumental and social skills)

$$\text{range: } 1: \geq 6\text{–}1: \leq 1$$

BEGINNING AUTONOMY

(about 13–24 months: moderately dependent with some mobility, instrumental skills, language comprehension, and speech; beginning social skills and toilet training)

$$\text{range: } 1: \geq 7\text{–}1: \leq 2$$

RELATIVE AUTONOMY

(about 25–36 months: relatively independent; considerable mobility, problem solving, language and social skills; daytime toilet trained)

$$\text{range: } 1: \geq 8\text{–}1: \leq 3$$

HIGH AUTONOMY

(about 37–48 months: greater independence, mobility and skills in all areas; prolonged periods of self-directed and sociodramatic play)

$$\text{range: } 1: \geq 9\text{–}1: \leq 4$$

GROUP DEVELOPMENT

(about 49–60 months: strongly emerging group awareness and regulation; further elaboration of all skills, especially language, abstraction, and sense of time)

$$\text{range: } 1: \geq 10\text{–}1: \leq 5$$

ORGANIZATIONAL CHARACTERISTICS

PROVISION FOR CONTINUITY AND DEVELOPMENT OF INDIVIDUAL STAFF-CHILD ATTACHMENT RELATIONS

LOW: No provision for continuity and development of individual adult-child relations. Most children handled by many adults without regard for individual child or adult needs and styles.

ADEQUATE: Each child assigned to one compatible caregiver part of each day for at least three months, or longer for those needing more care.

EXCELLENT: Each child assigned to one compatible caregiver several times daily for at least six months. Same caregiver is responsible for monitoring overall development (physical, cognitive, and socioemotional).

PROVISION FOR MULTIPLE ADULT-CHILD RELATIONS

LOW: Limited exposure to different adults, and always in the same fixed roles. No attempt made by adults to adapt to children's styles. Transitions may be sharp and sudden.

ADEQUATE: Moderate exposure to a number of adult caregivers in varying circumstances; some attempt to adapt to children's styles; few sudden or marked transitions.

EXCELLENT: Regular exposure to different adults in varying circumstances; sudden large transitions and traumatic relations carefully avoided.

CONCERN FOR BALANCE BETWEEN FLEXIBILITY AND STRUCTURE IN ACTIVITIES

Routines and Schedules: promoting adaptive flexibility, openness toward variation in experience, socially, cognitively, and with respect to time and space.

LOW: Little concern among the staff for balance. Written schedules reflect only rigid programming. Children and staff show signs of tension, inhibition, harassment, rigidity and/or disorganization. Activities tend to be either chaotic or rigidly overscheduled.

ADEQUATE: Definite staff awareness of balance principle evident in flexibility of written schedules and of the program, in discussions and in effort. Children and staff relatively spontaneous and free from tension. Activities and schedules are neither inflexible nor disorganized.

EXCELLENT: Emphasis upon balance prominent in continuing discussions and re-evaluations of methods and program effects on children. Well-defined written materials and guides used. Children and staff move, play, and work spontaneously and free from tension, yet with a definite sense of order, smoothness and purpose.

CAREGIVING-TEACHING STYLES

WARMTH AND RESPONSIVENESS

LOW: Few expressions of warmth and enthusiasm with respect to children's needs for attention. Important needs of children ignored for long periods of time.

ADEQUATE: Generally warm, positive, and friendly responses to children's need for attention; important needs of children are attended to expediently.

EXCELLENT: Frequent spontaneous expressions of warmth, enthusiasm, and friendliness with generally positive responses to children's needs for attention; children seldom left with important needs unattended for more than a few seconds despite competing demands.

PERCEPTIVENESS AND SENSITIVITY

LOW: No awareness of children's needs, frustrations, or problems. Problems dealt with in a punitive or nonaccepting manner; intervention shows lack of constructiveness and understanding; problems are not used as learning experiences.

ADEQUATE: Awareness of children's needs, conflicts, frustrations, and problems is apparent. Problem areas are usually handled directly and constructively through remedial intervention.

EXCELLENT: Perceptiveness of children's needs, conflicts, frustrations, and fatigue, etc., is everywhere evident. Difficulties are anticipated and sensitivity to the child's personal concerns and needs is shown. Intervention is preventative to minimize problems quickly and unobtrusively, using each problem situation as a learning experience for the child.

ADAPTIVENESS

LOW: No evidence of varying adult styles with circumstance or characteristics of individual children. Tension results when circumstances force change in schedules. Unable to deal constructively with multiple tasks, competing demands of children, or crises.

ADEQUATE: Some evidence of varying style with circumstances and characteristics of children. Adults usually adapt to changing circumstances, competing demands of children, multiple tasks, and crises with expedience.

EXCELLENT: Style varied according to the circumstances and characteristics of different children and rarely according to expedience alone. Adults adapt quickly, smoothly, and inventively to changing circumstances, coping easily and constructively with multiple tasks, competing demands of children, and crises such as injuries, social conflicts, large upsets of materials, etc.

FOSTERING AUTONOMY

LOW: Little awareness of a balance between child's needs for emotional support and autonomy. Children's conflicts, boredom, and frustration ignored or not dealt with consistently or constructively. Emotional support seldom designed in terms of individual needs.

ADEQUATE: Awareness of the need for both emotional support and development of autonomy. Children redirected to new activities when boredom, frustration, or conflicts arise. This is most frequently accomplished by changing the group's activities rather than individualizing a solution to the problem for any particular child.

EXCELLENT: Children's needs for emotional support and dependence balanced with encouragement of constructive, self-propelled play and activity through skillful supervision to counteract frustrations, boredom, or conflict. Children encouraged to find their own solutions to problems individually or cooperatively, with ample emotional support adapted to the child's needs.

FOSTERING COOPERATION

LOW: No encouragement of cooperative work or play. Teachers focus on activity of children individually except for arbitrary intervention to prevent or control disputes. Roles between children are seldom defined, and reciprocal relations and joint tasks between peers are not encouraged.

ADEQUATE: Children are guided to cooperate in work and play in well-planned tasks from time to time and cooperation is encouraged when opportunities arise in daily events. However, more cooperative interactions are between teacher and child than between peers.

EXCELLENT: Cooperative work and play tasks are frequently set up, including setting tables, setting out and putting away toys, etc. Situations and materials are inventively used to elicit collaboration, such as taking turns, defining and changing roles, reciprocal and joint action. Child-child interaction is fostered as often as teacher-child interaction. Children are shown how to guide one another.

PROGRAM SOCIAL GOALS

PROVISION FOR EXPOSURE TO ETHNIC AND CULTURAL DIVERSITY

LOW: Staff and children culturally homogeneous, no provision for the inclusion of either adults or children from different cultures; few culturally diverse information materials.

ADEQUATE: Staff and children representative of cultural diversity present in the community, or some effort made to include adults and children of different sociocultural backgrounds in regular attendance or through frequently inviting guests from different cultures to lead relevant theme activities; culturally diverse information, materials, and visits available as learning experiences from time to time.

EXCELLENT: Children regularly exposed to ethnic and cultural diversity among staff and children drawn from outside the community if necessary. Special guests from different cultures, information, materials, and visits utilized extensively in the program to teach cultural diversity.

EQUAL CONCERN FOR DEVELOPING PLAY AND WORK ETHOS

LOW: Little attention paid in staff discussions and procedures to the value of both work and play. Attention is limited to play and little consideration is given to developing interest in and responsibility toward work.

ADEQUATE: Continuing staff efforts to encourage varied and complex development of both play and performance of work tasks *with some success*. Staff and children's attitudes toward work and play not always clear or consistent.

EXCELLENT: Elaborate and extensive plans, procedures, and discussions to encourage varied development of play and work concepts and behaviors. The value of work and play are both presented *clearly and con-*

sistently in light of their contribution to both group welfare and cooperation and the development of the individual.

ENCOURAGEMENT OF FRIENDSHIP (PEER PLAYMATE ATTACHMENTS AND RELATIONS)

LOW: No evidence of efforts to foster friendship patterns among children.

ADEQUATE: Definite staff efforts to encourage healthy peer attachments with some success.

EXCELLENT: Children's interrelationships regularly appraised to encourage peer attachments based on complementary or similar personality traits, cognitive styles, and interests, to avoid unnecessary conflict and foster close playmate attachments in diverse ways, considering dominance-submissiveness, broad-narrow thinkers, gross-fine motor activity, etc.

PROVISION FOR DIVERSITY AND SEX BALANCE IN SOCIODRAMATIC (SOCIAL AND OCCUPATIONAL ROLE) PLAY

LOW: Almost no stimulation for sociodramatic play; no rearrangement of materials or coordination of play with story or musical themes or excursions. No sex balancing in activities.

ADEQUATE: Some regular rotation of settings and themes among different occupational roles (plumbers, doctors, secretaries, mechanics, etc.) and domestic roles; co-ordination of information themes, settings, and excursions. Definite attempt to alternate boys and girls among various roles.

EXCELLENT: Regular rotation and imaginative rearrangement of materials. Children encouraged to explore and develop many different occupational and domestic roles, with girls and boys cooperating with one another in tasks and settings. Traditional sex role stereotyping minimized. Sociodramatic play diversity enriched by thematic selection and presentation of information materials and records, coordinated with guided learning activities and excursions to occupational role and other settings over a planned time period.

PROVISION FOR REGULAR EVALUATION OF SOCIOEMOTIONAL DEVELOPMENT

LOW: Few, if any, organized and correlated observations of children. No discussions of ways to improve and individualize handling of children.

ADEQUATE: Periodic observations of different aspects of children's development, perhaps without well-defined scales or reliability checks. Some information from home available through parent involvement. Regular discussions on improvement and collective handling of children and the center, as well as providing suggestions for parents at home.

EXCELLENT: Regular systematic observation during play and other activities. Children rated on pertinent dimensions of socioemotional functioning such as warmth, autonomy, assertiveness, tension, peer attachments, cooperativeness, etc. Extensive cumulative records kept, including information about the child's home functioning through regular parent involvement. Frequent staff discussions on methods to further individual children's development, including interaction with parents or recommendations and guidance for further therapeutic aid given where appropriate.

Name of Center: _____
Address: _____
Phone: _____
Observer: _____
Date(s) of Observation: _____

				1 / 2 Low / 3	4 Adequate / 5	6 Excellent / 7	
Arrangement of Materials and Equipment		By types of activity	No organization by type				Careful organization by type
		By developmental level	No organization by level				Careful preparation by level
		Sequential arrangement	No organization by sets				Careful organization by sets
		Variability of arrangement	No regular rotation				Regular rotation of a good repertoire
		Ease of access	Poor display and accessibility				Careful display and good accessibility
Modes of Stimulation	**Quality of Guided Learning Program**	Frequency and regularity	Infrequent, irregular or with large groups				Regularly daily brief and extended sessions with small groups
		Quality and variety	Didactic, narrow or inappropriate methods of little scope				Comprehensive, with imaginative developmentally based methods
		Concreteness	Too abstract with few opportunities for manipulation				Concrete with active exploration
		Language stimulation	Language stimulation poor in all situations, either lacking or inappropriate				Language stimulation appropriate and rich in all situations
		Inquiry orientation	No encouragement of inquiry				Active program to elicit inquiry
		Imagination	Unimaginative stereotyped and structured sets of activities				Rich repertoire of learning: play and games used inventively
		Play orientation	Learning is formalized without the involvement of play				Learning is often play-oriented
	Free Play Program	Adequacy and frequency of free play	Few periods of supervised free play				Definite periods of well supervised free play
		Private play	No provision for private play				Regular daily periods for private play
		Fostering creativity	No attention to fostering creativity and construction				Systematic fostering of creativity and construction
	Excursion Program	Movement from center	No opportunity included in program				Elaborate program of community excursions
	Caregiving Routines	Routine care	Perfunctory				Routines used as learning experiences
	Evaluation		No systematic evaluation				Comprehensive program of cognitive assessment for program

Notes
(Comment also on particular strengths or weaknesses including any not covered by the scale.)

Form 4

Cognitive Stimulation Program

**ARRANGEMENT OF MATERIALS
AND EQUIPMENT**

BY TYPES OF ACTIVITY AND CONCEPTS

Arranging toys and equipment into categories to foster breadth and depth in concept development and types of play. Categories leading to possible areas of toy grouping are: free form creative materials, modular construction materials, structured means-ends (problem solving) materials, science and other information materials, record player, musical and rhythm instruments, sociodramatic and other role play props, large scale building materials, riding and wheel toys, climbing apparatus, etc.

LOW: Chaotic clutter or random piling of materials, without regard for harmony between types of play or stimulation.

ADEQUATE: Attention to division of materials and encouragement of diverse forms of play.

EXCELLENT: Careful, imaginative arrangement of all materials and equipment to foster diverse types of experimentation, construction, creativity, and sociodramatic role play.

BY DEVELOPMENTAL LEVEL

LOW: No attempt to plan or arrange materials according to developmental levels. Tidiness, when stressed, is generally irrelevant to children's needs.

ADEQUATE: Regular planning and rearranging of materials by age and ability levels.

EXCELLENT: Materials for all activities carefully arranged to match developmental levels. Complex and complicated materials regularly available for use under supervision.

SEQUENTIAL ARRANGEMENT OF MATERIALS

LOW: No sequential sets of materials available or maintained for specific concept-learning tasks (such as size, color, number, time, etc.).

ADEQUATE: A moderate variety of sets of learning and play materials sequentially graded in difficulty. Sets are maintained in moderate order and used regularly, sometimes with guidance.

EXCELLENT: A large variety of well-conceptualized and designed sequential sets; order is constantly maintained (except during use), and children are daily guided in their use in a variety of specific concept-learning tasks.

VARIABILITY OF ARRANGEMENT AND PERIODIC ROTATION OF TOYS AND EQUIPMENT

Recognition of principles of varying availability and arrangement of materials for purposes of novelty, to sustain interest and foster cognitive variability.

LOW: Arrangement of materials seldom varies: the same set of materials available each day.

ADEQUATE: Moderate attention to both a basic repertoire and regularity of rotation of some materials.

EXCELLENT: Good repertoire of basic materials for all important categories of play and learning; regular rotation of supplementary materials (toys, books, records) and equipment; varying selected information materials (pictures, books, records, sociodramatic tool props) often coordinated in a common theme embracing several areas of activity over a week or more.

EASE OF VISUAL AND PHYSICAL ACCESSIBILITY OF MATERIAL TO CHILDREN

Adequacy of type and arrangement of display shelves or other accommodation for materials and equipment intended for use during a given period, from small toys, books, and records, to wheel toys, climbing apparatus, etc.

LOW: Shelf spaces inadequate in number, size, and arrangement. Materials poorly displayed and difficult to reach (piled in boxes, stored in cupboards) or in a clutter on the floor, or shelves.

ADEQUATE: Fairly adequate shelf space and arrangement; moderate attention to visual display and ease of accessibility.

EXCELLENT: Careful arrangement of shelves in terms of number, size, height, and depth, with all unstored materials regularly and thoughtfully arranged to be visually inviting, uncrowded, easily scanned, identified, compared, and selected by children for play.

MODES OF STIMULATION

QUALITY OF GUIDED LEARNING: COGNITIVE GUIDANCE, TUTORING OR TEACHING

Actual guidance by adults or older children in play with children singly or in small groups, either as scheduled sessions or developed informally but purposefully in the context of free play.

FREQUENCY AND REGULARITY OF SESSIONS

LOW: Infrequent guidance by adults with toys, picture and story books, or musical material, either planfully or informally. If any sessions occur group size usually six to eight or more.

ADEQUATE: About three extended sessions daily of five to fifteen minutes or more or around five brief sessions of two to four minutes (average per child). Learning group sizes usually six or less.

EXCELLENT: Five or more regular extended sessions daily of five to fifteen minutes or more or many (10 or more) brief sessions of two to four minutes daily (average per child). Group size seldom exceeds five.

QUALITY AND VARIETY OF PROGRAM

LOW: Poorly developed program, if at all. Teaching methods are highly didactic, narrow, rigid, or oppressive; or loose, scattered, or vague. Material may be too complex, methods imprecise, or sessions disorganized.

ADEQUATE: Moderately developed and individualized program of some depth, variety, and flexibility.

EXCELLENT: Comprehensive, concept and skill oriented program, covering a diversity of topics with an emphasis on language, number, prereading (or reading), and perceptual-motor concepts and skills. Flexible and imaginative teaching methods, including play and peer interaction, developmentally paced and stimulating.

CONCRETENESS: SENSORY-MOTOR ORIENTATION

LOW: Little attention to demonstration of features and functions of objects, particularly objects found in everyday life and the immediate culture. Manipulation and active exploration of materials is discouraged. Explanations often inappropriate to level of development.

ADEQUATE: Teaching demonstrations include common objects and items from the immediate culture. Active exploration and manipulation of materials is permitted but not always encouraged. Moderate success in coordinating demonstrations of features and functions with appropriate verbal descriptions.

EXCELLENT: Stimulation is presented through simple demonstrations, particularly of common objects from the immediate culture. Active exploration and manipulation of materials is regularly encouraged. Simple language explanations are coordinated with features and functions, using materials appropriate to the developmental level and skills of the children.

LANGUAGE STIMULATION

LOW: Little recognition of the importance of language stimulation. Children frequently not talked to, or are talked at, rather than talked with. Routine activities often perfunctory and unaccompanied by explanations. When used, language is inappropriate to the developmental and skill level of the child.

ADEQUATE: Children talked with (rather than at) in many situations, with moderate enrichment of activities and routines by language. Verbal explanations common and usually fitted to the childrens' level and skills.

EXCELLENT: Language used generously, regularly, richly, and interpersonally with (rather than at) the children of all ages in all situations, especially in guided learning and caregiving routines. Language is almost always appropriate to the developmental and actual skill levels of the child.

INQUIRY ORIENTATION

LOW: Little attempt to encourage curiosity and inquiry among children in teaching activities. No attempt made to encourage understanding of tasks, problems, concepts, or phenomena.

ADEQUATE: Explanations regularly employed in teaching children; activities designed to provide information to children and teach concepts in a manner that arouses curiosity and inquiry into solving problems.

EXCELLENT: Learning activities typically approached by teachers or caregivers as fascinating problems drawing children and adults into collaborative inquiries about how things work. Tasks and phenomena are typically designed so as to be exciting to investigate, figure out, understand, and explain. Critical relations, key concepts, and clues used to guide children in explorations.

IMAGINATION

LOW: A standard, very limited set of concept-learning materials is available and typically used with little insight, and concepts are presented in stereotyped fashion. All teaching activities and basic care routines are presented routinely as necessary rituals, with little imagination or variation.

ADEQUATE: Materials and methods of teaching are selected and used moderately often in ways to stimulate the child's imagination in complex and creative use of the concepts and materials, even when materials are not extensive in number and variety.

EXCELLENT: A rich repertoire of learning materials is used regularly in grading learning activities formally and informally in an inventive and varied manner, using materials to arouse and sustain children's interest in learning, sociodrama, and creative activity. Similarly, inventive stimulation is provided in ordinary care routines, in part by employing imaginative variations in the tasks themselves.

PLAY ORIENTATION

LOW: When children are guided in learning, concepts are presented formally without manipulation or sociodramatic play. Examples may be insightful, clear, and even imaginative, but use of the examples for "irrelevant" social play or even for experimentation in manipulative play is discouraged. No extraneous play materials are offered or allowed.

ADEQUATE: Experimental manipulative play, sociodramatic play, and extraneous play materials and props are used moderately in teaching sessions.

EXCELLENT: Exploratory, problem solving, and sociodramatic play used freely in all teaching activities. Examples are used in many ways that are both playful and often imaginatively instructive. Extraneous props and play materials are used freely, but selectively to maintain interest in ways that extend learning.

FREE PLAY PROGRAM

Adequacy and frequency of free play program   Amount of time and quality of stimulation, care, and supervision.

LOW: Few definite periods of supervised free play. Children oversupervised in organized activity or ignored and neglected. No concern for toy availability, social density, conflict, constructiveness, persistence, diversity, or enjoyment.

ADEQUATE: Moderate provision for free play periods. Reasonably alert and stimulating supervision, encouraging children to select diverse activities, to experiment imaginatively and freely; attention to social density and conflicts.

EXCELLENT: Sustained periods of free play each day. High quality supervision provides a rich variety of types of play. Varied and imaginative facilitation of play to develop autonomy and cooperation, developing themes, group construction activities, social and occupational role play and a variety of problem solving and concept experimentation activities. Careful attention is given to group activity for cooperative, constructive or sociodramatic play to maintain proper densities and mediate conflicts quickly.

PROVISION FOR PRIVATE PLAY

Recognition of the need for individual play, without distraction or interruption, to foster development of personal and cognitive autonomy, concentration, reflectiveness, and persistence.

LOW: Virtually all activity is in the presence of a number of children. No provision for spatial separation.

ADEQUATE: Provision for most children to play for a few minutes alone several times a week.

EXCELLENT: Regular daily periods for each child to play alone in a small room or divided area of the playroom with an adult in viewing distance. Special methods used for encouraging children, especially those who are ordinarily hyperactive, hypersocial, overly dependent on adults, or who may already prefer periods of quiet and concentration, to enjoy playing alone.

FOSTERING CREATIVE AND CONSTRUCTION
PLAY DEVELOPMENT

LOW: Little or no attention paid to fostering creative and construction activities, even if appropriate toys are available. Available time overstructured with emphasis on stereotyped product rather than process and varying products. Children's progress in these areas is not followed or discussed with parents.

ADEQUATE: Moderate attention devoted to free exploration in creative and building activities. Attention is given to principles and products of creative activity. Discussions are held, parents involved, creations displayed, some products saved, and children's progress occasionally charted.

EXCELLENT: Systematic development of a setting, methods, and atmosphere to foster exploration and experimentation in depth of free-form (painting, drawing, or clay) and construction activities (building with blocks and other modular materials). Parents extensively involved and encouraged to foster creative activities at home, varying approaches experimented with;

competitive attitudes discouraged through fostering individual differences and encouraging cooperative projects; systematic records maintained, displayed and analyzed for use in guiding methods.

EXCURSION PROGRAM: MOVEMENT FROM CENTER

LOW: No movement from day care center or school except travel between home and center.

ADEQUATE: Moderate program of guided excursions, parent involvement, and attempts to link excursions with varying theme activities in the center's program.

EXCELLENT: Elaborate program of excursions to community facilities (stores, harbor, construction sites, factories, transportation facilities) and natural geographic sites (ponds, woods, fields). Visits are well planned to explore institutions in depth through repeated visits, correlated with interrelated and sequenced center activities and visits to related institutions. Extensive parent involvement and coordination with home planned excursions.

ADEQUACY OF DEVELOPMENTAL CARE ROUTINES

Feeding, eating, washing, toilet needs, dressing, sleeping, preparations, etc.

LOW: Routines treated as necessary tasks to be completed as quickly as possible, with little regard to child's acceptance or involvement in either accomplishing the task or learning. Children treated as objects, managed with few verbalizations; care characterized by coldness, indifference, or impatience and criticism.

ADEQUATE: Moderately regular warmth and involvement of child in learning and understanding. Regular use of language and encouragement of autonomy and cooperation among peers as well as with adults, where appropriate. Moderate balance between task accomplishment and personalization and learning.

EXCELLENT: Personalized and stimulating approach, with each occasion used as an opportunity for child and adult to interrelate warmly as well as learn a necessary task in which autonomy and cooperation are achieved through participation at the child's level of understanding. Children are systematically encouraged and shown how to help one another. Language is used freely and coordinated with activities, including poetry and songs, and novel objects to lighten the routine and expand the child's horizons. Excellent, variable balance between task demands and personalization and learning.

PROVISION FOR SYSTEMATIC AND REGULAR EVALUATION OF COGNITIVE DEVELOPMENT

LOW: No observations or assessments of learning or problem solving processes made.

ADEQUATE: General program of developmental assessment by tests or observations of selected competencies including language, general cognitive processes, and fine and gross motor skills. Parents are usually kept informed, and occasional information on home observations is obtained. Staff encouraged to suggest alterations to programs based on test results and observations.

EXCELLENT: A comprehensive program to monitor development in both group care and the home in a wide variety of areas including knowledge, language, problem solving, socioemotional, motivational, perceptual, and fine and gross motor skills, using both standardized and observational measures. Information is discussed regularly and used to construct an organized assessment to individualize methods and programming. Parents are kept informed in detail and regularly involved in planning and making use of assessments to further the child's development.

Environmental Profile

Form 5: Toys and Equipment

Name of Center: _____
Address: _____
Phone: _____
Observer: _____
Date(s) of Observation: _____

			Low 1	2	3	Adequate 4	5	Excellent 6	7
Indoor	Problem Solving and Creative-Construction Material	Construction toys: number of types	<2	3	5	6	7	9	>10
		Free from materials: number of types	<2	3	5	6	7	9	>10
		Structural problem solving materials: No. of types	<2	3	5	6	7	9	>10
		Structured materials: number of units per child	<.3	.5	1	1.5	2	2.5	>3
		Quality of all sensory-motor toys and materials	Poor					Ex-cel-	lent
	Information and Literary Materials	Total books, magazines and pictures: number per child	<1	2	3	4	5	6	>7
		Fiction books per child	<.5	1	1.5	2	2.5	3	>3.5
		Non-fiction books per child	<.5	1	1.5	2	2.5	3	>3.5
		Use of Public Library or parent circulating books: No. per child per month	<.5	1	1.5	2	2.5	3	>3.5
		Miniature objects and replicas: number of types (3 items per type)	<1	2	3	4	5	6	>7
		Objects and replicas: number of units per child	<.5	1	1.5	2	2.5	3	>3.5
		Quality of information materials	Poor					Ex-cel-	lent
	Props for Sociodrama	Number of types	<2	3	4	5	6	7	>8
		Quality of props	Few					Good	Many
		Number of units per child	<1:4	1:3	1:2	2:3	3:4	4:5	>1:1
	Physical Toys and Equipment	Number of types	<2	4	6	8	10	12	>14
		Number of units per child	<.3	.5	1	1.5	2	2.5	>3
		Musical and thematic value of record collection: Number of records per 20 children	<0	5	10	15	20	25	>30
	Gross Motor Toys	Number of types	<2	4	6	8	10	12	>14
		Number of units and sets per child	<.3	.5	1	1.5	2	2.5	>3
Outdoor	Hard Surface Play Area	Hard surface area equipment (check if appropriate surface)_____ Number of types	<2	3	5	6	7	9	>10
		Number of units and sets per child	<.2	.3	.5	1	1.5	2	>2.5
	Soft Surface Play Area	Soft surface area equipment (check if appropriate surface)_____ Number of types	<2	3	5	6	7	9	>10
		Number of units per child	<.2	.3	.5	.75	1	1.5	>2.0
	Natural Areas	Garden-nature area: number of varieties of plants	<2	4	6	8	10	12	>14
		Number of units or sets per child	<.3	.5	1	1.5	2	2.5	>3

Notes
(Comment also on particular strengths or weaknesses including any not covered by the scale.)

Form 5

Variety of Toys and Equipment

INDOOR

PROBLEM-SOLVING AND CREATIVE-CONSTRUCTION MATERIALS

Construction toys (Modular Unit Sets each having at least three pieces per child: miniature and unit blocks, building bricks, flannel boards, and various other combinatory construction, design, and theme materials—commercial and homemade)

range: ≤ 2 to ≥ 10 number of types of sets

Free-form materials (Moldable or free forming combinations; commercial or homemade, each having one set or unit of workable material for every three children: *Three-Dimensional*—clay, play dough, papier mache, toothpick constructions, etc.; *Two-Dimensional*—crayon and chalk drawing, finger and easel painting, collage, etc.)

range: ≤ 2 to ≥ 10 number of types

Structured (fixed and semi-fixed pattern) problem-solving materials (Jig saw puzzles—content configured, form boards, shape sorting boxes, size graded materials, color and number matching materials, containment-spatial relations materials such as various pans, boxes, and containers with assorted objects; infant-operated mobiles—commercial or homemade)

range: ≤ 2 to ≥ 10 number of types

Number of units per child Including all types (e.g., puzzles, container object sets, etc.)

range: $\leq .3$ to ≥ 3 per child

QUALITY OF ALL SENSORY MOTOR TOYS AND MATERIALS

LOW: Many unclear in design, poorly constructed, garish, or blurred in color; too many toys with hazardous features (sharp points or edges and fragile). Too many complicated toys (e.g., mechanical toys) offering few possibilities of constructive play for the age range.

ADEQUATE: Usually of good design, well colored, durable, and not dangerous. Toys usually meet children's needs for active manipulation and constructive play.

EXCELLENT: Most are of clear-cut design, many are imaginative. Simple well-balanced colors are used. Durable, safe and well designed to encourage active manipulation or constructive play.

INFORMATION AND LITERARY MATERIALS

Constant amount regularly available in each age group through purchase, libraries, and/or parent exchange.

Total books, picture magazines and pictures   Number *per child* (10 pictures = 1 book)

$$\text{range: } \leq 1 \text{ to } \geq 7 \text{ per child}$$

Fiction (picture story, poetry, etc.)

$$\text{range: } \leq .5 \text{ to } \geq 3.5 \text{ per child}$$

Nonfiction   (Crafts, knowledge of animals, agriculture, community life, etc.)

$$\text{range: } \leq .5 \text{ to } \geq 3.5 \text{ per child}$$

Use of public library or parent circulatory books   Number of children's books per child per month

$$\text{range: } \leq .5 \text{ to } \geq 3.5 \text{ per child per month}$$

Miniature objects and replicas   (Household items, clothes, tools, vehicles, boats, hardware, and electrical gadgetry, replicas of animal and plant life, etc.)

Number of types   (having > 3 items per type)

$$\text{range: } \leq 1 \text{ to } \geq 7$$

Number of units per child

$$\text{range: } \leq .5 \text{ to } \geq 3.5 \text{ per child}$$

Quality of information materials   (Books, pictures, and miniature objects)

LOW: Many unclear in design when realism intended. Highly oversimplified, poorly executed or overly complex designs. Poor in design or color; poor execution of intended imaginative designs. Little poetic or literary value in stories, maudlin, or overly aggressive themes. Designs and themes too often hyperfeminine or masculine and no consideration of ethnic and sex role diversity.

ADEQUATE: Generally adequate design, color, clarity, and execution of all pictures, book illustrations, and miniature objects. Generally good literary material with not too many aggressive or highly sentimental themes. Some inclusion of different ethnic groups and women and men in nontraditional occupations and roles. Few obvious stereotypes.

EXCELLENT: Uniformly high quality of all materials in design, execution, and of literary materials in themes. Nearly all are excellent in either realism or imaginativeness. Designs are rarely oversimplified and when complicated are still clear. Very few overly sentimental or overly aggressive designs or literary themes. No exaggeratedly feminine or masculine designs or themes; good representation of sex role and ethnic diversity in materials.

PROPS AND MATERIALS FOR SOCIODRAMATIC (SOCIAL AND OCCUPATIONAL ROLE) PLAY

Number of Social and Occupational Role Types

range: ≤ 2 to ≥ 8

QUALITY OF PROPS

LOW: Very few props and materials for stimulating sociodramatic play. A few items suggesting only domestic role play (tables, chairs, dishes, stove).

ADEQUATE: Several varieties of props, mock tools, and other materials for stimulating sociodramatic and occupational role play.

EXCELLENT: An extensive variety of props and materials, either commercial or homemade, for sociodramatic and occupational role play, such as office furniture, simulated factory machinery, store fixtures and equipment, kitchen appliances including stoves and sinks; adult clothes representing occupational roles; simulated tools of trades, ships, docks, subway stations, etc.

Number of units (individual props and pieces of equipment) and sets (where applicable, e.g., dishes, tools) per child—including all types

range: $\leq .5$ to ≥ 3.5 per child

MUSICAL TOYS AND EQUIPMENT

Number of types (Record players, Hi-Fi, and child-operable; tone, pattern, and pitch discrimination sets, commercial and homemade; bottles, bells, tuning forks, bamboo lengths, recorders, Carl Orff instruments, piano, guitar or other instruments—with staff to play; rhythm devices—commercial and homemade)

range: ≤ 2 to ≥ 14

Number of units per child—including all types

range: $\leq .3$ to ≥ 3 per child

Musical and thematic value of record collection (Number of classical, folk, jazz, and quality children's records for every twenty children; subtract from the total for each commercial "pop" record)

range: 0 to ≥ 30 per 20 children

GROSS MOTOR TOYS AND EQUIPMENT

(Climbing apparatus, riding, pushing, and other wheel toys, walking boards of varying widths; large hollow blocks, tumbling mats, swimming tank, trampoline, stairs, roller skates, tunnels, ramps, teeter-totter, climbing nets and ropes, swinging bars, etc.)

Number of types

range: ≤ 2 to ≥ 14

Number of units and sets (where applicable, e.g., skates) per child—including all types

range: $\leq .3$ to ≥ 3

OUTDOOR

HARD SURFACE AREA EQUIPMENT

(For use on asphalt, concrete surface areas): wheel toys—riding, pushing and carrying (trikes, bikes, wagons, kiddy cars, scooters, skates); hollow building blocks, boards, and manipulatable boxes; sandbox with water available, water play area, protected swimming pool; outdoor table(s), shelves, easels; workshop—carpentry, wire working; commercial and homemade.

Number of types

range: ≤ 2 to ≥ 10

Number of units and sets per child   (where applicable, counting ten hollow blocks and other pieces of modular materials as a set)

range: $\leq .2$ to ≥ 2.5 per child

SOFT SURFACE AREA EQUIPMENT

(For use on soft surfaces—lawn, sand, sawdust, dirt, tanbark): climbing apparatus, slides, climbing rope and nets, swings, rocking horses, teeter-totter, bridges, tunnels, walking boards, ramps, trampolines, hammocks; socio-dramatic play equipment—stores, play houses, simulated (stationary) boats, trains, cars, trucks, factory, office, etc.—commercial and homemade.

Number of types

range: ≤ 2 to ≥ 10

Number of units and sets per child   (Where applicable counting five walking boards and other modular pieces as a set)

range: $\leq .2$ to ≥ 2.5 per child

GARDEN-NATURE AREA

(Species of trees, shrubs, plants, flowers, etc.)

Number of varieties of plants of all types

range: ≤ 2 to ≥ 14

Number of units (trees, shrubs, plants) and sets (where applicable, e.g., flower beds) per child

range: $\leq .3$ to ≥ 3

Index